LOVE LETTERS TO MESSIAH

Modern-Day Psalms

ADAM ZINSSER

Love Letters to Messiah: Modern Day Psalms
Trilogy Christian Publishers
A Wholly Owned Subsidiary of Trinity Broadcasting Network
2442 Michelle Drive, Tustin, CA 92780

For information, address Trilogy Christian Publishing
Rights Department, 2442 Michelle Drive, Tustin, CA 92780.
Trilogy Christian Publishing/ TBN and colophon are trademarks of Trinity Broadcasting Network.
For information about special discounts for bulk purchases, please contact Trilogy Christian Publishing.

10 9 8 7 6 5 4 3 2 1
Library of Congress Cataloging-in-Publication Data is available.
ISBN 979-8-89041-589-9
ISBN 979-8-89041-590-5 (ebook)

DEDICATION

This first book, and I say first because God has told me that there will be many more to come, is very special to me. So first and foremost, I would like to dedicate this book to my Lord and Savior, the true lover of my soul, Jesus Christ of Nazareth. I offer this book, along with my life, as a holy and living sacrifice. May my actions, prayers, and words be holy and pleasing to Him. He is not only the author and finisher of my faith; He is also my everything.

Next, I would like to dedicate this book to the greatest gift that God ever gave me, my beautiful and precious daughter, Gia'Ann Nicole Zinsser. This book is special because I was incarcerated my daughter's entire life, and I don't know how to love her like she needs and deserves to be loved. Yet Christ is teaching me day by day how to love with a pure love, and I look forward to being able to love my daughter, help her, and show her the love of Jesus Christ. The thing I regret most about the years I spent in prison is missing my daughter's life, not being there and not being the father that she deserves. This book is in honor of my daughter, Gia. I pray that she will read it and see that Christ changed my heart and that I am here for her now. Not only that, but also that I will never leave her again. I love you, Gia, and I'm proud of the excellent young woman you have become. I pray that you learn from my mistakes and excel to greater heights. You were created for greatness. Keep reaching for the stars and know that I am immensely proud of you.

The next person I am dedicating this book to is my mother, Judie Zinsser. You are absolutely amazing. You have sacrificed so much for me and my brother, Michael. You have lived a life of total service and sacrifice. Your personality and character reflect the ways of Christ so much. I just never saw it because I didn't know Jesus. I want to thank you for your never-ending love, for your belief in me, and for sticking by me through all the hell that I put you through. I hope that from this day forward, I will continue to make you proud. I hope you know that I honor you in all that I do. I can never even explain to the world what you did for me. But I know, you know, and Christ knows. And He honors you for all you have done for me. And I honor you too. I love you Mom.

The last dedication I have is to my brother, Michael Patrick Zinsser. I want you to know that I love you, and I pray for you every single day. You are a warrior, and I know that you are fighting for your life. I know because I was there with you. I know it's hard, and I pray every day that you will trust Jesus and allow him to give you new life. I will always believe in you, always love you, and always be here for you. I want you to know that Jesus loves you so much, and you are everything to Him. You also mean the world to me. I know you will win this fight and you will change so many lives, Mike. Just keep fighting and know that I will never leave you nor forsake you ever.

I pray you all enjoy this book and know that it is nothing but love, love to Christ and from Christ. God bless you in the name of Jesus Christ.

ACKNOWLEDGMENTS

I would like to take the time to acknowledge my partner, Donna Lambert, for all the legwork she put in. She helped me find a publisher, cheered me on, retyped all my poems, and gave me so much wisdom during the process. I am also grateful to her and her husband, Rod Lambert, for all they have done pouring into my life. I consider them my second set of parents, and I am very grateful for their presence in my life.

I'd like to acknowledge my big brother, David Rose, for all that he has done to pour into my life spiritually, and just for being a wonderful friend and role model that I very much needed as I made my transition back into society.

My pastor, Eugene Kitney, for being the great man of God that he is, teaching me to walk deeper into my calling with Yeshua.

I'd like to acknowledge each and every person who has ever taken the time or put forth the effort to encourage me and build me up in my faith as I walk with Messiah. I love each one of you in the mighty name of Yeshua of Nazareth.

God bless.

INTRODUCTION

This book has been a long time in the making in my heart. When I found Jesus Christ, He completely changed my life, not on the outside, but from within. When I first encountered Christ, I was completely broken and felt like my life was over. I had been to prison four times, and I was on my way back again. I was strung out on meth, living by the needle, and was completely shattered. So my conversation with Jesus went something like this: I don't believe You care about me, and I don't really believe that You even know me. But if You are real, then show me a miracle. You show me a miracle and I'll walk with You. I didn't hear back from Him right away. But what happened is, He made the miracle. From darkness to light, from a drug-addicted gang member to a son of God with a vision. I can never explain to you what Messiah did for me. He literally transformed me when I never thought that it could be done. Jesus taught me to love when I never understood it. He taught me how to respect myself and how to respect others. He taught me integrity and how to build instead of tear down. He taught me to speak life instead of death. He made me fall in love with Him like I never fell before. I'm not going to lie; I've been chasing Messiah with all my heart since then.

I'm not a perfect Christian, but my heart for Messiah is pure. He said, "Blessed are the pure in heart, for they shall see God." And since Christ took out my heart of stone and gave me that heart of flesh that was promised in the book of Ezekiel, and then gave me a new spirit, I've never been able to stop chasing Him. He gave me the spirit of King David and the spirit of Elijah. I chase Him like David. I romance with Him with my words, and I speak about all things to Him, the good, the bad, and the ugly. I like to look at my writings as modern day Psalms in a sense. My goal for this book is that my words will help others to express and identify their feelings toward God, so that through these writings, you may draw closer and closer to Messiah.

One of the greatest promises God ever gave us is in Jeremiah 31:3 (NKJV). What He said was this: "I loved you with an everlasting love so I drew you to myself." I pray that God the Father, through the work of the Holy Spirit, will touch my words, anoint them, and use them to draw each and every one of you that read this closer to His Son, our Lord and Savior, Jesus Christ. Walking with Christ is a love affair, not a set of rules and regulations. He is a judge of the heart. Knowing that, we need to allow Him to steal our hearts and dive deeper into His waves of love. Jesus was never looking for a bunch of miserable robots who all think they can please Him by following the law to the "T." No, He was looking for children that He could love, protect, walk through the good and the bad with and teach them to overcome. But He wanted that love and affection to be reciprocated. That is what it's all about.

So as you read these poems, please open your heart, and allow God to show you His love. The glory has always belonged to Christ. Yet so often we rob Him of what was always His. I pray that through this book, we can begin to bring Him His glory once again.

For Thine is the kingdom, Thine is the power, and Thine will forever be all the glory.

TABLE OF CONTENTS

When I was a child, I spoke like a child and did childish things.
I was excited about my future and all that it brings.
I knew I'd been hurt and had a really tough past.
Yet for all I had been through, I didn't think it could last.

The problem with being a child is you don't see what is real.
Every day's an adventure, but it's all how you feel.
I never understood that I was born into addiction.
And I couldn't foresee all the upcoming affliction.

So I made the mistake of thinking I knew
That the sun was always shining, and the skies were always blue.
I got hooked on the drugs and then I lost my mind.
Twenty-four years in prison, but my mind I'd never find.

I hurt so many people when I was blinded to the light.
I was angry and simply tired, for my whole life had been a fight.
I didn't know the answers but I couldn't take correction.
And when I looked in the mirror, I was disgusted with my reflection.

I finally gave up and raised my hands in the air.
I gave it all to Jesus and asked Him if He cared.
He wrapped his arms around me, and He looked into my face.
He said, "I've got a special gift for you and it's called my grace."

I went from gang life to Christ life, from prison life to being free.
I learned that I am special, that there's only one of me.
So now I walk with Jesus, my losses became wins.
You may see tattoos, but He died for all my sins

When I was a child…

Adam Zinsser   15

It takes the darkness to appreciate true hope.
You have to be broken to lay down the dope.
The depression gets heavy, and conviction is strong.
You feel like you're drowning, like it's all going wrong.

Life begins spinning way out of control.
Inside you're shattered and yearn to feel whole.
You just can't make sense of the life that you're living.
There is no remorse, there is no forgiving.

This is the price of the places we've been.
It's a life of enjoying the pleasure of sin.
It pulls you down under, and it never lets go.
But all of this pulls us to the one name to know.

See, we have to be lost to realize we're found.
It's like being deaf all your life and then you hear sound.
The sound that I speak of is the voice of pure grace.
It fills you with hope and makes your heart race.

I speak of the voice that heals you inside.
The voice that will tell you that He heard when you cried.
That's why I'm grateful that I lived through the night.
Because I met the Son and then He gave me sight.

From darkness to light . . .

Some people will know the pain that's inside.
It's a pain that's so great for a part of me that died.
You see, I died to my sin, but it's still chasing me.
It's like I want to do right, but the sin won't set me free.
The battle is spiritual, but it's mental, too.
It's a battle we all fight, that's me and that's you.
See, Christ gave his life so we could all live.
Yet when it comes to one's self, it's too hard to forgive.
The pain cuts so deep that inside we are dying.
There are so many nights where we just lay in bed crying.
Thinking of the ones that we left shattered and broken.
Wishing we could take back those words we had spoken.
Love is a puzzle, and the pieces are scattered.
We come to Jesus broken, we lost all that mattered.
He says ashes to beauty is what He will make.
But we get this new heart and we are scared it will break.
You see, this is the life when you carry the Cross.
You have to move on from the things that you lost.
New heart, new spirit, and looking above.
You see, Jesus is teaching us a new definition of love.
For God so loved the world that He crucified His Son.
His love is never ending, but He wonders why we run.
The pain is still inside, but He'll take it all, it's true.
This is why He died, to unbreak me and you.
Christ-like life, it's hard, but it's worth it.
Jesus loves you.

The Pain That's Inside...

ADAM ZINSSER

There are times I've looked back at the things that I've done.
The battles I've lost or I thought I had won.
I think of the sadness and all of the pain.
I can't help but wonder, just what did I gain?

I tried and I tried to always get better.
When my mother left me, I tried not to let her.
I never just chose to live life to get high
Or waking up every day just wanting to die.

I've been broken and shattered, then broken again.
My whole adult life was spent in the Penn.
Twenty-four hours locked away in a cage.
Inside I was eaten by my anger and rage.

You see the tats and you're so quick to judge.
I want a fresh start, but you still hold a grudge.
I'm covered in the blood of that sweet precious Lamb.
I'm the son of a king, the great I Am.

I went to the Cross, and I was crucified with Christ.
I wasn't born once. See, now it's been twice.
Because I'm a new creation that was saved by His grace.
So please think of Jesus when you look at my face.

Because I've been forgiven.

I worship You because You are the best ever to live.
I worship You because You died so the Father could forgive.
You're perfect, You're strength in the depth of my weakness.
You taught me love, but also true meekness.

You showed me a way when I just couldn't see.
You hung on that Cross because of Your love for me.
So like David, I'll praise you with all that I am.
I shout to the heavens that I worship the Lamb!

The Lamb without blemish that came to eradicate sin.
You paid the price for all broken men.
I worship You for the way You changed me inside.
For You are the groom, and I am part of Your bride.

I worship You in love for all that You did.
Because You are my fortress, it's in You I am hid.
From everlasting to everlasting, I give You the praise.
I'm asking You to teach me to number my days.

So I may forever worship You!

I love You Messiah...

I'm doing something new. Do you not perceive it?
Your fire isn't burning, so your fire I have lit.
I'm making a pathway through the wastelands I need you to see.
You've been blinded by the world, but now you'll see Me.

Before I do this, I'm telling you what I've done.
Just like it was prophesied before I sent my Son.
Old things have passed, but all things become new.
This is how I work, and I'm doing it with you.

So come now, let's reason, though your sins are like scarlet.
See, my people are unfaithful, and they act like a harlot.
They worship money and things that in the end only perish.
But I offer you a gift that I promise you'll cherish.

I sent all my prophets as a warning before the fall.
I hung my Son on that Cross as the world's final call.
You see the physical, not by faith, not by sight.
Yet when I send my Son back, He'll be like a thief in the night.

So hear Me, My people, and repent of your ways.
Just like my servant Moses, learn to number your days.
For the time has drawn near where I shall be seen.
So worship me now and stop looking for grass that is green.

My name is Yahweh, and I created this.
I told my servant Paul to greet with a holy kiss.
Listen to my words and surrender, for I am good.
For soon it'll be too late, then you'll wish you still could.

"Thus saith the Lord, I make all things new. Do you not
perceive it . . ."

Yahweh Said This . . .

Most people don't know the way that I feel.
You hear me speak of Jesus, but you think it's not real.
You think that this Christ-like life is all done by works.
You really became a Christian because of the perks.

You try to reach perfection in living out the Scriptures.
Your legalistic mind is painting all these pictures.
You condemn how I walk or the way that I look.
You don't worship the Author because you're worshipping the book.

You say you walk in love, but you judge your fellow man.
You say you trust in God, but you're veering from his plan.
You fast and you pray, but you only walk by sight.
Yet the faith you claim is not shining like a light.

My relationship with Jesus is deeper than you know.
No matter what you tell me, His love just makes me glow.
He holds me by the hand and pulls me through the deep.
The waters that I speak of are the tears from when I weep.

He loves me oh so deeply with my tattoos and my flaws.
His love that flows right through me, it calms them, and it draws His children to salvation, for blessed is this tree.
They think that they see Jesus, but it's Jesus that's in me.
I am His reflection.

He Is I and I Am Him . . .

Dear Jesus...

You are my everything, and this much I know,
That in the times I fall short, You make sure I grow.
You show me greatness where I just saw shame.
You prove that there's power and strength in Your name.

You fill my heart up with joy and such gladness.
You hold me so tight when I'm drowning in sadness.
You catch all my tears in a bottle that's Yours.
You open my heart so I can see heaven's doors.

I love you so much that my heart wants to bust.
You taught me loyalty as well as to trust.
You took Your word and made it flesh within me.
Then You hung on that Cross just to set my soul free.

So this is my letter to profess all my love,
To sing with the angels as they worship above.
Saying thank you Lord Jesus for making me new
And for showing me a love that is faithful and true.

I love You Messiah...

And I will forever worship You.

Most people don't understand just who you are.
That most of my life you had to love me from afar.
From hospitals to rehabs, from prison to the streets.
You've not seen many victories, it's been mostly defeats.

But through it all, you have loved me like no one else would.
When I wanted to give up, you made me believe that I could.
You told me to stand when I just kept on falling.
You kept me focused when the devil was calling.

I thank God for a mother that believes like you do.
I thank God that your love is so patient and true.
You are the reason that I'm even here.
You proved time and again just how much you care.

So these are my words to give you my love,
To just honor you as well as my Father above.
I love you and I'm grateful for all that you've done.
You're the world's greatest mother and I'm proud to be your son.

I love you, Mom!

Love, your son... Adam Zinsser... a miracle of God!

There are so many things that take my eyes off You.
The things of this world that I thought were all true.
I know in my mind Your laws are spiritual and good.
That's why I try harder, but You knew that I would.

Your love is like a drug that I can't help but chase.
In my heart I'm always hidden in Your secret place.
I meditate on the things that are written in Your Word.
I keep my eyes on the sky, waiting on that heavenly bird.

I need You so much that it kills me inside.
I look at that Cross and wish it was me who had died.
I can't help but imagine the things that You went through.
I just know in my heart that I truly love You.

I loved You yesterday and today, and it'll be stronger tomorrow.
I love You because You took away all my sorrow.
I realize You've shown me the error of my ways.
So now I shall follow You for the rest of my days.

I choose You over everything that I thought was so great.
I simply choose to love, and I reject all the hate.
I pray that You use me to shower the world with Your love
And take as many as I can when I come to meet You above.

I simply choose You, Jesus.

Yeshua of Nazareth . . .

The name that shall forever be above all other names.
The very one that made me grow up and quit playing games.
It's true I was a child, but I just didn't want to grow up.
I was like a cancer. I made other people wanna throw up.

I stole, and I gang-banged. I hurt, and I lied.
I robbed, and I sold drugs, and I know too many died.
I was full of the anger, the hate, and the greed.
When someone hurt my feelings, I'd make them bleed.

I was a soldier of darkness. Satan had my mind.
I never knew that real love was understanding and kind.
Most people will never see the things I saw as a little kid.
Most nights I was starving, all alone as I hid.

Broken and in pain, my whole life was just a lie.
It's sad since your birth, you're on a mission to die.
But then I met Messiah, the One who's simply love,
Who's powerful and just, but precious as a dove.

He held me oh so close, and He healed the scars within.
He told me that He loved me, and I'd never be broken again.
He taught me all His ways, and He brought me back to life.
He gave me inner peace, and He took away the strife.

So this is just my way of worshipping His name.
For purifying me and freeing me from shame.
I thank You, Jesus Christ, for You hung and said it's done.
I'll worship You forever, and this is signed . . . your son.

I worship You, Yeshua . . . I will forever worship You.

ADAM ZINSSER   25

I've always been different, never really fit in.
Not talking about here, but rather places I've been.
My whole life I struggled just trying to be accepted.
Doing so many stupid things, but I guess that's expected.

From foster homes to hospitals, the streets, and then the Penn.
Losing my sanity trying to prove myself to men.
Life was always breaking me and never showing me grace.
I hated myself so much that I tatted up my face.

I was born into depression with no soul around to tell.
People spoke of heaven, but I was stuck in hell.
This was life to me. It was all I really knew.
It's living by the motto — "to thine own self be true."

Then I met this man who told me He was God.
He told me He'd been with me when I had been abroad.
He told me that He loves me, and He looked into my face.
Then He touched me in my fear and showered me with grace.

Now I walk with Jesus. I was lost but now I'm found.
I was deaf to the voice of Jesus, but now I hear His sound.
I'm living for his glory and walking in His ways.
Some like to call it redemption, but I say it's better days.

See, I'm walking with Jesus.

Where you seem to see weakness, I only see strength.
I see a Savior who went to great lengths.
You see vulnerability, but I see great meekness.
Cause I'm really a lion, and I don't have weakness.

I carry this cross for the ones who are broken.
I treat you with kindness with my words that are spoken.
You wanna see me die, but I wanna see you live.
You hold on to grudges, but I say let's forgive.

The anger that's in you is killing you inside.
Yet I walk in humility with peace and no pride.
You wanna judge me for things that I've done.
But I left your sins on the Cross with the Son.

You prey on my downfall, but I help you stand.
I'm spreading the gospel across all the land.
You speak of death, but my words are life.
I speak of peace, yet you speak of strife.

You want the drama, and you want to fight.
You live in the darkness, but I walk in light.
You chase that money, but I chase the king.
You glorify hatred, but it's God's love I bring.

You're chasing fools' gold and just always stressing.
Yet I rep the kingdom and speak of God's blessing.
I love you enough to always be there.
Cause I'm repping Jesus, and you should know that He cares.

There's no greater love than what He did for you.
So I'm spreading His love to show you it's true.

Just to die to yourself and then start forgiving.
Because that, my friend, is when you'll really start living.

There's no greater love than His love for you.

He said, "Follow me, and I'll make you fishers of men."
You'll hear it, receive it, not be the same again.
I'll change how you think and even how you see.
Because it'll become more about God but less about me.

We are all born separated from God.
We search for the answers here and abroad.
We find all these things to fill up that hole.
Yet we run from the Savior, the true love of our soul.

We try to do good things and love those around.
But the world just blinds us till we can't hear the sound.
That sweet, soft voice that is calling our name,
Yet we sit there confused as we drown in our shame.

I love because first it was God that loved me.
But it's the Jesus in others that I try to see.
Because He is the creator of all that's been made,
That's saved and unsaved, it's His life He'd trade.

So I heard that call, and I chase after Him.
I worship His name so my light won't go dim.
This is the mission of the sheep who've been chosen.
For the ones who have seen Him and whose hearts are not frozen.

We minister the love that He showed on that Cross.
We help others find wins where there had been loss.
We shine His bright light in a world that is broken.
Then we live out His gospel and the words He has spoken.

Because we are fishers of men.

ADAM ZINSSER   29

In the precious name of Jesus, I come to You with a humbled heart.
Thanking You for this new day and a brand-new start.
Asking You to hold my hand as You guide me through these deep waters.
Asking for wisdom to guide Your precious sons and daughters.

Teach me how to love them like only You can.
Help me to find the broken ones who saw You and ran.
Open my eyes and blow upon my spirit.
Whisper my name so only I will hear it.

You are the one who gifted me with life.
So now I ask You to grant me a good wife.
Allow me to move in love and affection.
But when the world looks at me, let them see Your reflection.

The daily bread that I ask for You is Your Holy Son.
The One that hung up on that Cross and whispered, "It's done."
Lead me not into hardship, and keep me from temptation.
For You have made me a royal priest of Your nation.

So I call on Your name in tenderness and love.
Allow me to be faithful until I join You above.
For You are my everything, and it's a must that You see
That in this heart of mine it's only You and me.

I shall preach from the mountain tops and worship Your name.
Because ever since You touched me I've not been the same.
I just can't stop chasing You, not now and not ever.
Because Thine is the kingdom and Thy glory forever.

I love You. I need You. And I sit here in tears.
Just thanking You forever for erasing my fears.
I worship You, Father, and I carry my cross.
Because everything else to me is nothing but loss.

You are my Forever, and this is my prayer to You.
Asking for the strength to always stay true.
Through the good and the bad may my faithfulness last.
And may I always look forward and not ever in the past.

I'm a product of the Lamb, but don't forget the Lion.
I'm from the new tribe of Judah and there ain't no more trying.
I don't have to say certain things or walk like most do.
Cause when the Lion walked out of that tomb, He said He was through.

I live by His strength, and I walk through His spirit.
The Lion within me is roaring; do you hear it?
I'm trampling the serpents that are under my feet.
I'm rebuking Satan as he drowns in defeat.

I'm allergic to religion and all the world's games.
I only scream, Jesus. I reject all other names.
The blessings that are out there are mostly fools' gold.
I'm wiser to deception as I've gotten so old.

You may think that you're living, but is your walk truly real?
Is your salvation by faith or just something you feel?
Cause emotions are a weapon from the enemy to strike.
Jesus is relationship. He's love, not just like.

I walk as a soldier whose cause is for Christ.
I wasn't born once, but with Christ it was twice.
My sword's in my hand, and my crown's on my head.
I serve a God that is living, not a God that is dead.

I serve Jesus Christ of Nazareth.

You found me when I was broken, shattered, and so lost.
I was lost inside the needle, and I didn't know the cost.
My mind had gone to nothing, had demons in my head.
I'd stick the needle in me just wishing I was dead.

The voices that would haunt me were telling me all these lies.
The nights I walked the streets were haunted by my cries.
The pain inside was deep, and I couldn't stop the bleeding.
The drugs were only killing, but I couldn't stop the needling.

I couldn't find the strength to put the needle down.
I couldn't lose my pride and at your feet lay them down.
I couldn't seem to find the will to wanna live.
I couldn't find it in me to ask You to forgive.

Then You came and held me close there to Your chest.
The needle in my arm, but then You gave me rest.
You told me that You loved me, and then You set me free.
The drugs no longer had me. I saw You on Your knee.

This was my last time ever getting high.
Now I'm living for You and no longer want to die.
So this is just a thank You for all You did for me.
Cause ever since I met You, I've been happy as can be.

Thank You, Jesus...

Jesus is the one who delivered us from sorrow.
He's the very one who is the Author of tomorrow.
He's reason when it's crazy, and He soothes the soul.
He finds us broken in pieces, yet then His love makes us whole.

He is a healer but also conquered defeat.
One thing I've learned is He's the true Mercy Seat.
He'll never let us down, and He'll always lift us high.
He saves our tears in a bottle when we cry.

He's the only one who ever loved us enough that He'd die.
When I think of how He saved me, my only question is why?
He is my portion, but He's also my Lord.
I carry the word that He gave me as a sword.

The Cross was the greatest love letter the world's ever seen.
He even made me lie down in grass that was green.
He showed me true wisdom, and He blessed me with grace.
He gives me the strength to keep on running this race.

It's true, love's an action, but there's just so much more.
It's also a Person. See, it's heaven's door.
The Person I speak of is our God up above.
What I'm saying is Jesus is the definition of love.

For if you do not know love, you do not know God, for God is love.

My path is a path of great resistance.
It's the reason I'm asking for assistance.
For when I am weak, You are strong.
It's like with me, You make the song.

But the notes that come forth, they must be of You.
For You are the one they call faithful and true.
So I sing for Your chorus. I bask in Your grace.
To the world that is broken, I show them Your face.

From the valleys to the mountains, and all through the skies,
I preach Your sweet gospel, and I tell of the prize
Which is heaven and peace, it's joy in one's heart.
It's repentance of sin and a new fresh start.

For You are holy, and You are true, and You are my God.
I shall scream hallelujah from here and abroad.
I love You, Lord Jesus. With You I have won.
So when asked who I am, I tell them I'm God's son.

Forever saved by grace.

Some don't understand just who I am.
I'm a true son of God, a product of the Lamb.
I'm as gentle as can be, but don't mistake it for weakness.
It's humility with strength. Jesus calls it meekness.

I'll encourage you and teach you, and love you for sure.
I can't get you into heaven, but I'll show you the door.
I'll pray for your life and hope things get better.
And if you ever get lonely, I'll write you a letter.

See, I'm the son of a King. His name is El Shaddai.
If I told you God's not real—well, I'd be telling you a lie.
He is real, and He's living, but it's true He was dead.
It was only three days, they wrote about it in red.

It's true I'm His servant, yet I'm also His priest.
To me, He must be the greatest, and I must be the least.
He's my Savior, my hero. But He's also my friend.
His name is Jesus Christ, and I shall worship Him till the end!

I love You, Jesus 4-ever!

I remember the first time that we ever kissed.
But now I look back on all that I missed.
The first time we met, you stole my heart.
Little did I know that you'd tear me apart.

You told me you loved me and that you truly cared.
That you treasured the moments that we had shared.
I held you so close and gave it all up for you.
But look at the hell that you put me through.

I gave up my family and even my daughter.
She needed me, yet I never got her.
I let you in my heart and even in my veins.
No wedding, no music, just the sound of trains.

It was nothing but lies and hurt in the end.
Now hearts have been broken that may never mend.
They say love is patient and that it's been kind.
But the love that we shared, I'd hate to rewind.

I'm writing to tell you that there is not an "us."
See, I gave my heart and life to Jesus.
You took me to ashes, ruins, and tears.
I wish I had never met you or wasted those years.

So I gave my life to Christ.

So long and good riddance.

I want to thank You for loving me from heaven.
Hallow out this day like You did it on day seven.
Give us this day our daily bread.
And wash me with Your words that are written in red.

Lead me not into temptation, but deliver me from the one
That's been a liar from day one and went against Your Son.
I know that he sees me with my head down.
Yet I rebuke him in Your name as I give You my crown.

I thank You for this day of life that You have given.
I thank You for the Cross since I am forgiven.
I lift up Your name as high as I can see.
I'm simply here to thank You for just choosing me.

You are my redeemer, my God, and my friend.
I'm simply here to worship You and that's till the end.
I'm humbled by Your love, and I wanna see Your face.
But mostly I'm just thanking You for all Your precious grace.

So Thy will be done in my heart as You see fit.
Keep my flame on high, and make sure it's always lit.
For Thine is the kingdom, the power, and all the glory.
For You are the Author, and I'm just Your story.

Amen and amen. I love You, Jesus.

I am the clay, but God is my Potter.

I come to You to repent of all my sins,
For the wrong things I've done that I viewed as wins,
For those I offended and those that I hurt,
Especially the ones that now sleep in the dirt.

I ask that You heal me of all fleshly ways.
I ask that You show me the way to see better days.
Wash me of the sin that is killing me inside.
Show me I am worthy, and that it's the reason You died.

Show me the power that is in Your Resurrection.
Teach me to rid myself of my many imperfections.
Allow me to love others the way You love me.
And give me the understanding so that inside I'm free.

Walk with me, Jesus, and help me overcome.
Let my love reach the masses and not only some.
Breathe Your spirit upon me so I can reach all my brothers.
Make it less about me and much more about others.

I bow to Your greatness, and I give You the glory.
I'm humbled and honored to be a chapter in Your story.
For Thine is the kingdom, and the glory is Yours.
Forgive me, Christ Jesus, for I see heaven's doors.

Amen . . .

Everybody needs somebody, and that definitely includes me.
After spending my whole life in prison, it tends to be hard to see.
Sometimes it's easy but then other times so hard.
I want to know people, but it's hard to let down my guard.

My trust is in Jesus, so I walk in the spirit.
Yet each time I fail it's like—well, that part I'll fear it.
Yet I realize His love, it casts out all fear.
So I felt like it's important that I write this and share.

It's hard to do decades, then come out and live.
When you've always been taking, it's hard to learn how to give.
When you've never trusted, it's hard to give trust.
When you've always been addicted, being sober's a must.

This life is a challenge, it's a hill I must climb.
It's not quite as easy as making words rhyme.
Yet my life was chosen by the Man on the Cross.
So anything minus Jesus to me is a loss.

But easy it's not, and I've got to keep fighting.
I have to keep helping others with the words I am writing,
And pray that maybe someone will feel what I've said
And maybe one day be touched by the words written in red.

Because He saved me...

People often wonder if Jesus is real.
Faith is to them based on what they can feel.
They are walking by sight, but there isn't any trust.
But see, when walking with Jesus true faith is a must.

Faith is believing in things you can't see.
Faith is just knowing God's got you and me.
Believing in His goodness no matter how it may look.
Faith is the key to unlocking the book.

Thousands of promises that with faith will come true.
Faith is the goodness of God that's for you.
It's nothing to see but just what God knows.
As the promises come true, your faith surely grows.

Remember that faith alone pleases God.
Yet walking by sight is not faith, it's a fraud.
So trust in God's goodness and rest at His feet.
For when your faith is true there won't be defeat.

We walk by faith...

The Lord is my shepherd, yet what does this mean?
And what exactly are the pastures that are green?
To me, those pastures are His Holy Scriptures.
It's His laws in my heart becoming permanent fixtures.

It's walking out His ways and praising through the storm.
It's rejecting what the world considers as the norm.
It's prayer and meditation, not alcohol and drugs.
It's ministry and love, not gang life and the thugs.

It's knowing that He's there and not looking for a feeling.
It's humbling myself and worship while I'm kneeling.
The pastures that are green are safety, and they're trust.
It's the best love that I know, not merely just the lust.

See, He made me a shepherd, yet I'm still just a sheep.
For I read in His Scriptures, for me He would weep.
So I'll lie down in these pastures and watch Him up above.
For the pasture, to me, is simply resting is His love.

He makes me lie down in pastures that are green,
And it's the only true love that this heart has ever seen.

Just a sheep in His pasture.

You are the potter, and I am Your clay.
It is You I depend on as I walk through this day.
You're strength in my weakness and sight where I'm blind.
It is You that I seek, and it's You that I find.

I give myself away in hopes of tasting You.
I minister Your teachings, for they're tested and true.
I know of Your greatness, and I know what You did.
And I know when You called me, like the first one, I hid.

But that was the old me and this is the new.
I'll worship You and praise You in all that I do.
I'll lift up Your name, and I'll march up that hill.
But when I hear You command me, that's when I'll be still.

The gift You have given is not simply life.
It's a peace that's inside that is minus the strife.
It's a chance to exceed the lies and limitations.
To have a relationship with You, minus all the imitations.

So I stand here before You, humbled and broken.
My heart is now pure after reading all You have spoken.
Just walk with me, Jesus, and let me minister Your love.
And whenever You're ready, just take me up there above.

For I am yours forever...

I decided to wake up and just write y'all a letter,
Especially the ones who think life's supposed to get better
When you lay down your sins right there at Christ's feet,
Because you're tired of hurting and tasting defeat.

What I want to tell you is that the struggle is real.
That Satan tends to drive you off the way that you feel.
And life isn't always going to simply excel.
You still have your problems, but there's Someone to tell.

Your anger will be there, the sadness will too.
But greater is He that is inside of you.
This walk that we walk, it's mostly uphill.
With a cross on our shoulder, and it's hard to be still.

You must trust in the work that Jesus has done.
You must worship in the storm, and believe you have won.
You take comfort in the blood that Jesus has shed.
And walk this by faith through the words written in red.

Easy, it's not, but worth it for sure.
For heaven's your destination and Christ is the door.
But it hurts and it's hard, and it's not what you feel.
It's simply believing by faith that He's real.

This is Christ life!

I am the light of this world while I am in it.
I created the earth with My finger, and I spin it.
I made you in love, and it's My spirit in you.
I created the trees and the skies that are blue.

You were created for a purpose, it's true.
When you hear My voice, you'll realize you knew
That from the beginning, your purpose was love,
That your final destination is with me up above.

I am the One who has brought you this far.
To me, you're as precious as the brightest star.
When you trust in Me and obey My commands,
It brings me so much pleasure, and I heal all the lands.

Know that I am with you in all that you do,
That I'll never leave you or forsake you.
I'll teach you My ways and make you My light.
For those who are blind, I'll give them all sight.

This is My gospel that I've given to you.
These are my promises, which always come true.
See, you are My child, you're not just My friend.
And remember, I'm with you all the way to the end.

For I am the light of the world!
And you were created to
Let Me shine through you!

Love Always,

Jesus Christ.

Always remember that He is much greater
Than any potential enemy or your biggest hater.
He's light in the darkness and warmth in the cold.
He's greater than any weapon that has ever been sold.

There's no power that's greater than Christ that's within.
He defeated Satan and even paid for our sin.
He became the curse, so we'd become the blessing.
Then He hung on that tree so that we could quit stressing.

He's a lion and a lamb. He's God, but He's a man.
He's not just our Savior, but He is the plan.
The price that He has paid is paid for all time.
He was hung up there to die as if He had done the crime.

The gift that He offers is the strength to overcome.
Yet He offers this to all, not merely just to some.
So surrender your will to the One who gave it all.
And stand firm in your faith and walk worthy of the call.

1 John 4:4

I'm just grateful to be forgiven.
I'm not quite at the point where I can say I'm living.
But one thing I can say, I'm totally surrendered.
Because I've counted the cost of His services rendered.

I mean, they kicked Him, they punched Him, they spit on His face.
He died for us all, the whole human race—
The ones who are killers or the ones who are blind.
He just asks us to seek, and we're promised to find.

The ultimate gift which is life everlasting,
If you can't hear His voice, then you should try fasting.
Then take His hand and feed off His spirit.
You take on His yoke and His love, well, you share it.

For the ways of this world will just leave you broken.
It's like you're trying to breathe, but you're always choking.
Yet Messiah gives life, He gifts us with breath.
So what will you choose? Choose life over death.

Choose life over hate, and instead of anger, compassion.
Choose to rep Christ, not the latest fashion.
Carry your cross, share the burdens of others.
And if you really love Christ, help your sisters and brothers.

As for me, I'm forgiven.
I choose to live . . .

You left the ninety-nine and made me the one.
It's like the love of the Father for His only Son.
You came, and You took me over Your shoulder.
Just like I was young, even though I was older.

You washed me and held me in grass that was green.
Unlike any true love that I'd ever seen,
You showed me the passion that I'd never felt.
With my life, You knew the hand I was dealt.

You taught me Your ways and showed me such grace.
Your smile was kind when You looked in my face.
You told me You loved me and knew I was hurt.
You showed me the heavens when I was stuck in the dirt.

Now I walk with You, and I give You my all.
I realize now I had always been called.
Now I'm a shepherd on the hunt for that one.
To show them the love of God's only Son.

Thank you, Jesus!

I want you to realize that the power's in the Resurrection.
He had to die for our sins, but in His rise is perfection.
Many were hung up there on that cross.
Jew after Jew, it was loss after loss.

But what separated Jesus from all the rest
Is that He would rise up and prove He's best.
He's the only One to empty the tomb.
He walked straight out of there like it was no more than a
womb.

In a way, that is where eternity was born.
It's the power Paul needed to be rid of that thorn.
The thorn that pierced him right through his side.
But that's the love of Jesus, for He died for his bride.

So feel the Resurrection as it turns through your veins.
And then watch your many losses be transformed to gains.
You become strong in your weakness and you stand up so tall.
And His grace will resurrect if you ever do you fall.

So remember the Cross, for it's the price that He paid.
But remember the promises in which He had made.
Because they all became true when He walked free of that grave.
It's only the name of Jesus that has the power to save.

Thank you, Jesus!

I want to live off the power of Your Holy Spirit.
The things that You teach me, well, I just want to share it.
I wanna heal all the broken and help the blind see
That it's really Your spirit that's living through me.

I wanna collapse all the walls that keep others in.
And wash them in Your blood to free them of sin.
For the ways of this world only leaves people broken.
Let me open their ears to hear the words You have spoken.

I believe in Your goodness as well as Your power.
I'm a watchman on the wall as I look from the tower.
Just waiting to see You, for You'll come again.
I live for Your glory, not the pleasing of men.

You gave Your life to allow me to live.
You taught me the blessings, not to receive but to give.
So thank You for life and the spirit inside.
You see, I never started living until I had died.

I need You, Jesus!

When I was in prison, God gave me a vision.
He told me I would preach, but there would be division.
He said I would get rejected like all of the others
The prophets—that is, by my sisters and brothers.

He told me He'd make my life in a book,
That He'd show the world just what Satan took.
The good and the bad, the heartbreaks and loss.
Just like He showed His Son on the Cross.

He made my life story into a lesson He'd teach,
That it's not just the words or the things that we preach.
That the power of God shows best in the pain.
For you can't see the rainbow without all the rain.

He told me the lessons were in the midst of the wars.
That He'd show the world how He opens the doors
That you never thought possible, the ones that weren't seen.
He said He'd make pastors from junkies and fiends.

So my life is a story but a lesson as well.
It's a victory story of a soldier who fell
But raised back up, as a righteous man could.
Yet four years ago He said in a dream that I would.

And I said, "Here I am Lord."

I pray that when you hear me, it's His love you feel.
I know that when you see me, it's to Christ that I kneel.
When I'm weak, He is strong, and His light will shine through.
I pray that you feel Jesus in all things I do.

The path is not easy, but for me there's no choice.
As a sheep in Your flock, I live for Your voice.
I chase all Your promises and stand on them all.
I call on Your name in times that I fall.

I rest in Your love, and I bask in Your grace.
I rest in Your word that I'm in a heavenly place.
For You are my future, I've let go of my past.
One thing I know is that this bond will last.

You are the Potter and I am Your clay.
You are the bread I must eat each day.
So I bow to Your greatness and give You my praise.
As I walk right with You for the rest of my days.

I worship You forever!

He wipes every tear that falls from your eyes.
He knows all the names of the stars in the skies.
He gave it all up so you'd have the chance
To live in abundance, to laugh, and to dance.

He is the Lamb that went to the slaughter.
When the bride had collapsed, it's His love that got her.
For His love is the greatest and won't ever fail.
That's why it's to Jesus I surrender and kneel.

The Word became flesh and walked up that hill
With a Cross on His shoulder while they shouted, "Kill."
He hung on that Cross, then took His last breath.
For the wages of sin can only be death.

Though He never sinned, He'd still pay the price.

That's why to know Him, you must be born twice.
Once by the water and then by the spirit.
And then when He calls, I promise you'll hear it.

The promise is forgiveness for that which you've done.
To become God's daughter or even His son.
To walk in the victory that's free of the shame.
I speak of Christ Jesus, for there's no other name.

That saves you...
He'll wipe every tear.

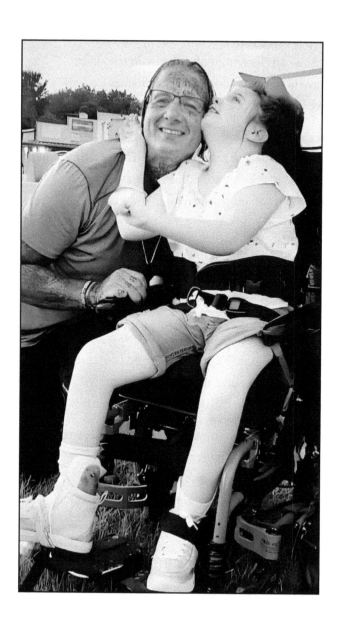

LOVE LETTERS TO MESSIAH

I think of the depths of God's beautiful love.
And the way that the angels just watch from above.
But then I'm reminded there are angels down here.
And it reminds me how much God really cares.

This is God's angel, and I want you to meet her.
Her name is Christen, so let your heart greet her.
She was born with limitations, but look at her smile.
She stacks all of God's kisses way up in a pile.

If she can find joy in each day that she's here,
And she never complains how life's just unfair,
Then what can we learn from the way that she lives?
Such a beautiful soul that just loves and forgives.

She is the reason that I am able to fight.
She keeps God's heartbeat right there in my sight.
Her laughter, her smile, not to mention her love
Just shows you that angels are down here and above.

Remember that angels are real!

You knew of my wounds and my damage inside.
You knew that I failed, but in my own way I tried.
You saw all the trauma that had damaged my mind.
And You came in my heart knowing just what You'd find.

I was a vase that had been dropped from the shelf.
I hit the ground and shattered, chasing power and wealth.
I made myself God and rejected your ways.
I mocked the true Christian that was humble and prayed.

Yet You saw the disease that was killing me.
You knew I was blind even if I could see.
You knew I was damaged and that it wasn't fair.
You saw that my heart of stone could not be repaired.

Your greatest promise is that You make all things new.
Eight thousand promises, and they all came out true.
So You touched my spirit and breathed on my soul.
And what had long been shattered, well, it then became whole.

So this is my way of worshipping You
For all that You've done and continue to do.
To tell You I love You and I need You so much.
And to let the world know that I was healed by Your touch.

By your stripes I was healed.

Today is a day of gratitude.
You changed my life and even my attitude.
You taught me to smile and no longer frown.
I'm walking on water where before I would drown.

The ways of the world just have no appeal.
And You taught me salvation is not something I feel.
You healed all the scars that cut me within.
You told me you were present in the places I've been.

With Your wings spread around me as I saw everyone dying,
You said You heard my tears fall each time I was crying.
You showed me the bottle that held all my tears.
You said perfect love, well, it casts out all fears.

You showed me that Cross where You won the battle.
You picked me up and put me back in the saddle.
You gave me a vision of preaching Your words.
You taught me the names of the stars and the birds.

Then You told me You chose me at the beginning of time.
And that You gave me the gift to make all my words rhyme.
The glory is Yours and I give it to You.
Because Your love is the best my heart ever knew.

Jesus, I love You...

The fire inside me just will not go out.
The spirit within me, it just wants to shout.
To wake up this world, for they all lay asleep.
To tell them of Jesus, to get on their feet.

Your words that are in me, they show me the way.
When I don't understand things, I get down and pray.
I ask You for guidance and wisdom as well.
I thank You for grace that saved me from hell.

I bury Your laws so deep in my heart.
I rebuke all the things that tear us apart.
For You are my Savior that keeps my lungs breathing.
The thing I fear most is the thought of You leaving.

Breathe on my spirit and walk with me slowly.
Put Your hand on me and make me feel holy.
Let me lie down with my head on your chest
To just feel Your love and just know that I am blessed.

I love You, Yeshua...

My God is my shelter in times of distress.
He found me broken and my life such a mess.
He picked me up right there off the ground.
I was shattered and deaf, for I heard not a sound.

He opened my eyes, and He opened my ears.
He held me so close, and He wiped all my tears.
He told me He loved me and knew of my pain.
He spoke to the sky and stopped all the rain.

He showed me my worth and exposed all the lies.
He said I wouldn't start living till the old me dies.
He showed me the Cross and just how He did it.
He said He knew of my sins, but I still must admit it.

He took me out in the waters, way out in the deep.
He knew I was sad and said, "Go ahead and weep."
He told me to trust Him and let Him inside.
Then I hung on that Cross and the old me died.

Now it is Jesus that's living in me.
I preach to the broken and help the blind see
That He is true life, and He's heaven's door,
That when you're walking with Jesus, there's always more.

This is my story...

Yes and Amen!

Over eight thousand promises, and they all became true.
You're the Word become flesh, and it's all yes in You.
Peace and tranquility, love, and such grace.
And when this race is over, I will be kissing Your face.

I know that You've got me, and You won't let go.
I know that I need You, and I need You to know
That You died for me, through You I live.
You taught me to love, to understand and forgive.

Not just with others, but also myself.
You taught me your laws, such spiritual wealth.
You showed me such kindness, trust, and compassion.
Walking with You is true satisfaction.

I want the whole world to know just who You are.
I want them to feel close and not ever afar.
The ones that are blind, won't You please let them see?
Then transform their lives like You did it with me.

My faith rests in You cause I know that You're real.
I don't walk this out by the way that I feel.
I trust You in hardships and even in sorrow.
I believe in Your power of a better tomorrow.

So do what You will in this heart of mine.
Fill me up with Your spirit so my light will just shine.
Make me an example of a promise come true.
As I continue to honor You in all the things that I do.

I love You, Jesus!

You had told me to be strong and courageous!
What You didn't tell me was that it would get outrageous.
But You told me don't ever be scared or afraid.
As I walked in the desert just searching for shade.

Then I was drowning in those deep, deep waters.
Surrounded by Jezebels but searching for Your daughters.
I was weakened by drugs that coursed through my vein.
I felt like You had forsaken me as I went insane.

Murder all around me, lives were being taken.
Overdoses everywhere, lives were forsaken.
The devil in my head telling me this is it.
My legs burned from standing, but there's nowhere to sit.

My God, my God, what have You done?!
Suddenly a voice said, "I've never left you, my son."
You came and stood over me. You blew on my spirit.
It was a heavenly sound in my heart. I could feel it.

My strength was restored, and then I could see
The legions of angels that were all around me.
I thought I was lost, for I had heard not a sound.
Yet now I was standing, and I knew I'd been found.

I said, You are my rock, my shelter from pain.
That to live is for You, but to die is my gain.
For then I'll be one with the One who made me whole.
The one who restored all that Satan had stolen.

You are with me always.

I worship You.

ADAM ZINSSER

A New Song...

The God that I serve is a God who provides.
The ways of this world, well, it only divides.
You see, the wages of sin will always be death.
For each person it's different, but for me it was meth.

But greater is He who is inside of us.
For He has a name, and that name is Jesus.
He takes all the things that are broken and shattered.
He makes them all new because to us they all mattered.

He shows us the things in our hearts that are wrong.
Yet as a master musician, He writes a new song.
We call it our life, but He calls it bliss.
He blessed our hearts with a heavenly kiss.

We were blind, now we see. We were deaf, now we hear.
We see that His love—well, it casts out all fear.
We rejoice in His goodness, and we spread out His love.
We bring others to Jesus as He watches above.

This is the journey that He wants us to make,
Cause the ways of this world are merely heartbreak.
So just take a moment and give God Your praise.
Then live out his next song cause it's called Better Days.

Yes, Jesus Loves You!

For The Bible Tells You So!

Jesus Is the Plan!

I used to live my life trying to figure out a plan.
Instead of trusting God, I put my faith in fellow man.
I had ups and I had downs, but I never seemed to grow.
My life was stuck on stupid, but I didn't even know.

One day Jesus told me He had a plan for my whole life.
He said, "Son, I want to rid you of the madness and strife."
He told me I was backwards, that the world would let me down.
He said, "Son, I made you royalty, and for you I have a crown."

He washed me of my sins, and then He fed me from His word.
He blew on my face, and then I saw that precious bird.
Slowly all my ways began to change by the day,
The way I treated others or the words that I would say.

My plans went out the window cause now He gave me sight.
His ways became my ways, and I was shining with His light.
See, Jesus simply showed me that He truly is the plan.
And that I am filled up with His spirit.
For He made me a new man.

Jesus doesn't have a plan. He is the plan.

The Lord is my rock, as well as my shelter.
He introduced me to lady wisdom and I know I felt her.
She showed me things from the past that I'd seen.
Then showed me that in this broken world there's no grass that is green

God is the One who breathes life in me.
He opened the eyes of my heart so I could see
That the things that are shiny are not always gold.
That if I build my house on sand, in the storm it shall fold.

The Lord guides me in the darkness with His voice as my light.
He strengthens me with His spirit so I'll win this fight.
He shows me things that I never knew from the start.
He cleansed me of my sin and gave me a new heart.

It's true I still have sadness from the things that I've done.
But I gave it to the Father when He gave it to the Son.
So this is my declaration of the One who gave it all.
I love You, Christ Jesus, and I've answered Your call.

God has a way of bringing us through the deepest waters.
He grooms us and prepares us for His most beautiful daughters.
He takes us through things that would break most men.
Then right when you can't stand it, He says, "Now do it again."

I did all my life behind prison walls,
Always sweating commissary and depressing mail calls.
Just wanting to be free but not understanding this,
That if you leave prison without God, there's so much you will miss.

Two decades and a half is what I gave away.
Doing drugs and gangbanging, but never did I pray.
I sold my soul for lust, and that was for the game.
Yet I would end up in a cell just drowning in my shame.

Then finally I surrendered, and I gave it all to Christ
The fifth time doing time, not just once or twice.
I was tired of the heartbreak and all the tears I shed.
I was tired of even living. I felt like I was dead.

But Jesus came and saved me, for He sets the captives free.
Then I went back to prison, but this time repping me.
I walked through prison's gates but then walked out still on fire.
I simply went on in there to rep my true Messiah.

To say it's good on this side of Jesus!

ADAM ZINSSER   65

For God so loved the world that He gave His only begotten Son
So that whoever shall believe in Him, the victory has been won.
You were blind, but now you shall see
That greater is He who is in you as He is in me.

Think about your losses or the heartbreak you've had.
Then think about all the things that have ever made you sad.
Then lay them at His feet along with your sins,
And just watch all those losses be transformed into wins.

For the Word became flesh and walked this earth as a man.
But Romans 8:28 states that it was all a part of His plan.
The foolish became wise, and the weak became strong.
And through His precious spirit you see right where you saw wrong.

See, there's no greater love than that Lamb that's a Lion.
He finished the work, and I promise I'm not lying.
So rest in His love and walk in His glory.
Surrender to His ways and let Him rewrite your story.

Because the Cross was a gift from the heavens above.
It was a letter from God titled . . . "This is my love."
Just rejoice in His grace and allow Him to show
That His spirt is all you need in this life to grow.

For God so loved the world . . .

I'm Redeemed!

I've been in the lion's den, and I was dead in the grave.
I denied the Lord Jesus or His power to save.
I shot dope and packed guns, and I was soaked in such hate.
I was full of false pride, and I thought I was great.

Yet he who exalts himself shall always be humbled.
I was brought to my knees as the skies all just rumbled.
Like Paul, Jesus asked me why I persecute Him.
Then, like Paul, I was blinded and my whole world went dim.

Yet three days later the scales were peeled from my eyes.
A new creation was born as the old me just died.
I carried that Cross, then I hung on that hill.
Then Jesus took me off it and said, "Peace be still."

My heart of stone was removed, and I got a heart of flesh.
My spirit was renewed, and everything was fresh.
I was chosen for a calling to tend to all His sheep.
Like Peter, I was broken. I denied Him and I weep.

But here I am a new man, full of mercy and His grace.
My body is on earth, but my spirit's in a new place.
A place where all is peaceful, and I'm seated by His side.
And Jesus said I'm worthy, and it's for me He had died.

I'm redeemed by His love . . .

ADAM ZINSSER

Why would I fear the enemy when I walk with You?
Why would I be ashamed of Your laws when I know You are true?
Should I run from the devil, or should I stand with the sword?
I say, I'll walk up that hill with my cross made of boards!

For You are my shelter from all of my pain.
You are my ark when I face all life's rain.
You are my healing from all my hurt.
Your breath resurrected me from my grave in the dirt.

I claim victory in You, and I scream out Your name!
I dunk myself in Your water, and I wash off the shame.
I am on Your path, and I bask in Your light.
I was born to be Your warrior, and I'll be here to fight.

You see, Your Word became flesh when You entered me.
I'm screaming hallelujah since You set my heart free!
I'm standing firm in my faith as I always chase You.
I only want to praise You in everything that I do.

So walk with me, Messiah, and show me Your love.
Give me all Your blessing as I worship You above.
For I am Your servant, but I'm also Your son.
As I hear Your precious voice, it's to You that I run.

Yes, I will worship You forever.

This is my way of saying things will get better.
It sounds like a poem, but it's really a letter.
To tell you how much you own my heart.
Just praying one day we'll get a new start.

I know that I hurt you being gone all those years.
I know your anger was born from your tears.
You have a right to be angry, for I was gone for so long.
But what I really was hoping was to write a new song.

Time has gone by and life keeps on going.
But now it's different seeds in which I am sowing.
The seeds that I'm planting are ones of God's love.
And He makes them grow right there from above.

I want to unbreak all that's been broken.
I want to take back certain words that I've spoken.
But I want to say things that I never did say.
Like, each night I cry whenever I pray.

For you are my sunshine, but you're also my soul.
Without you in my life I'll just never be whole.
This is my letter saying I hope you're not sad.
I send with my love, and it's signed, "Your Dad."

I love you...

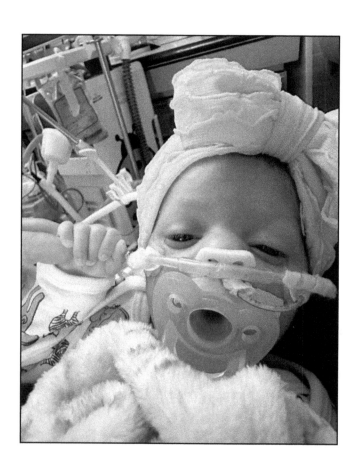

LOVE LETTERS TO MESSIAH

Today I want to say a prayer for this beautiful baby.

Everything is yes with Christ Jesus. There's not ever a maybe.

I want to lift this little angel on up to God's throne.

And ask Jesus to touch her so she won't feel alone.

Touch her, Messiah, and let her know that she's chosen.

But also melt the hearts of the ones who have been frozen.

You know this is Your gift to a world that is shattered.

Show them the power of the only touch that ever mattered.

Breathe on her spirit and raise her in glory.

I believe in Your goodness and I trust in Your will.

Just heal her entire body while she's quiet and still.

Thy kingdom come and thy will be done.

I'm bowing to Your greatness and I'm asking as Your Son.

Give her the strength she needs to walk this life out.

I'm here in sackcloth and ashes, and it's Your name I shout.

You are the Healer of all that's been broken. I'm calling You on Your promise, the very words that You've spoken.

You know my heart, and You know how I feel.

So raise this child up and show the world that You're real.

I need You, Messiah.

Sometimes we think we know what is best.
Like all doors are God's door since we know we are blessed.
We roll the dice, but God makes them land.
It's infinite knowledge we can't understand.

This is where faith in God becomes real.
To trust in Christ Jesus and learn how to kneel.
To cast all our worries and bask in His grace.
To know that He's God and stay in our place.

Satan will try to rule our emotions.
He'll try to disrupt us as we go through the motions.
But faith is just trusting that God will come through.
It's holding His hand in all you go through.

Faith without works is faith that is dead.
With five loaves of bread just look who God fed.
He made sure His children had all that they need.
This is the reason on the Cross He would bleed.

The trick is to trust in all that God does.
To know He's the greatest that there ever was.
To trust in His ways as He shines His light.
It's walking by faith and never by sight.

This is our journey...

I bow my head to the One who had chosen
To die for my sins, and on the third day He rose.
To the One who is life, but He's also light.
The light of the world who in turn fought my fight.

He found me in pieces that were scattered around.
Yet He collected them all right there off the ground.
He blew in His hands that held what was broken.
He then said the most beautiful words ever spoken.

He said, "All things are new, and you are my son."
He said, "I've paid for your sins, and I said it is done.
So walk in the victory that I've given you,
And believe in my promises, and they'll all become true."

From darkness to light, from sorrow to joy,
To a true son of God, from a scared little boy.
This is the reason I give Christ the glory
You see, He chose to make me a miracle story.

So I will forever bow my head to Him in reverence.

ADAM ZINSSER   73

When you ask me or wonder who I used to be,
My only response is just look and see.
I was broken inside, and the world broke me down.
I never knew how to smile, there was only a frown.

In my earlier years I never knew love.
I had to steal just to eat when push came to shove.
That led me in a direction I never wanted to travel.
Instead of life getting better, I'd just watch it unravel.

Foster homes, abuse, to gang life and the Penn.
I knew I'd die young, I just didn't know when.
Drug use was escape from all of life's pain.
The hospitals I went into were for going insane.

It's like being stuck in a blender, and the speed is on high.
The pain's so intense I just wanted to die.
My last trip to prison I gave Jesus a chance.
I broke down in tears but He said we'd dance.

He showed me His ways, and He washed me within.
He taught me His grace, it wipes out my sin.
He gave me a robe and wiped all my tears.
He proved that His love would crush all my fears.

It took me a while to learn who I am,
To change from a wolf to a purified lamb.
But look at the pic and see how He did it.
From a dope fiend, to a prisoner, to a light, and He lit it.

This is my story that He wants me to tell.
He wants you to know that He saved me from hell.

This is the power of the true Resurrection.
When you come to Christ Jesus, He'll show you perfection.

From ashes to beauty

He makes all things new.

What He did with me

He'll do with you.!

Thank You, Jesus!

Many people think that the struggle's too much.
That's only because they've not felt the touch
Of the One who created all that's been made.
Through Him we excel, succeed, and get paid.

The struggle is real, but the victory is there.
The power of the Holy Spirit overcomes any fear.
You give it to Jesus, cast your cares at His feet.
Then walk into victory and stomp on defeat.

I've been down, I've been broken, but now I'm standing tall.
Every time I was hopeless or felt I would fall
He caught me and showed me the strength that's within.
See, the struggle's much deeper than our life of sin.

It's facing all the madness that life throws our way.
It's trusting in God's plan and remembering to pray.
It's walking by faith and not just by sight.
And when the world's bucking Jesus, it's doing what is right.

You must trust the process and trust in God's ways.
No matter how tough it is, expect better days.
You lift up His name and glorify Him.
And keep your light burning so it will never go dim.

This is Christ-life...

I started out in the projects eating on these bricks.
My mama gave me up to do H and turn her tricks.
I never had direction or family to call my own.
I got stuck in that blender, and I'd never really grown.

Then I turned to hustling and sold bricks as clear as glass.
Meth is what they call it, but the glory never lasts.
From Juvie to the Penn, from rehab to the streets.
I was fighting for a victory, I got nothing but defeats.

They teach you that the game will be so good to you.
They teach you that the streets will always be so true.
But everyone I knew is now dead or in the Penn.
The motto that we lived by was "get it how you can."

Twenty-four years in prison is what I gave the game.
But then I found my Jesus, and I've never been the same.
I'm building up a future, and I'm living for His name.
No more living shady, and there's no more feeling shame.

From bricks to bricks, to building for this kingdom...

ADAM ZINSSER

One thing that I've learned is that life is just so crazy.
There's never time to waste or sit around and be lazy.
You get up every day and you give it to Him.
For He's the tree of life, yet we are just a limb.

We keep our eyes focused on those things up above.
We help our fellow neighbors, exemplifying love.
The gospel that He gave us is simply how we live.
Whenever we're offended by others, we forgive.

We are the light in the darkness and life where there's none.
We're simply mirror images of the Father and the Son.
The spirit that lives in us will show us all the way.
You ask Jesus in your life, then the spirit will always stay.

It's Christ-life I speak of, it's all I've come to be.
See, you're really hearing Jesus, yet looking straight at me.
He has given life and grace on top of grace.
The sacrifice was made, for on the Cross He took our place.

So the life I live for Jesus is all I have to give.
It's me that you are seeing, but through me Christ now lives.
I'm hoping that you hear me, and let my Messiah in.
Cause otherwise you're dying as you drown there in your sin.

I'm just in love with Jesus . . .

I want to thank You for being the Father You've been.
For keeping me from killing myself way back when.
When I was lost in my sin, and I was blind to the Cross.
You kept Your arms around me when I chose to be my boss.

You created me from nothing, but You made me great.
You delivered me from sickness, the anger, and hate.
You were patient and kind, and You never stopped forgiving.
If it wasn't for You—well, I would have never started living.

I was lost and so broken, yet You put me back together.
So now I am chasing You, and I will be forever.
You took all my sorrows, and You turned them all for good.
And I won't even lie, I never thought that You would.

But now I'm Yours, and I'm proud to be Your son.
The adoption was official when You hung and said, "It's done."
You taught me love when all I knew was hate.
You found me in the trash, and You're making something great.

I'm thanking You for being there when push came to shove.
I'm thanking You for teaching me the meaning of true love.
The message that I'm sending or what I really wanna say
Is simply that I love You and Happy Father's Day.

Because You are my everything!

ADAM ZINSSER

79

I study to show myself approved.
I prayed, and the Holy Spirit moved.
I gave thanks for all that Christ did for me.
Because I was a blind man, yet now I can see.

I see the heavens open up, and the Son is looking down.
He's wearing white robes, on His head He wears a crown.
His eyes are like fire and His tongue like a sword.
He's the reason I am breathing, He's my King and my Lord.

The Scriptures I have buried deep down within.
Like water, they wash me of all of my sin.
I wear Christ like a robe each day I wake up.
I ask the Holy Spirit to fill me up like a cup

I'm sold out to His ways, it's really all I know.
He washed my heart clean, now it's like softened white snow.
He taught me things about faith and true love.
So even as I sit here, my eyes look above.

I can never really tell you what He has shown.
Yet as I've studied His Scripture, my faith has just grown.
He shows me things that I just never knew.
So what I'm trying to tell you is this: Christ-life is true.

He's the only One...

You will forever be my everything.
It was You who said, "Death, where is thy sting?"
You made the walls of Jericho fall.
You hung on the Cross, and it's the world You would call.

You were God and a Man, a Man and a Lion.
For the ones who deny You, I know they are lying.
You are life, but You're light, You're peace, and You're love.
I'm in sackcloth and ashes, praising You up above.

I see all You do, and I'm simply in awe.
I know You created me, and I have not a flaw.
I need Your thoughts as my thoughts and Your ways my own.
It's for You I press forward and forget the chances I've blown.

You are my fortress, and I take refuge in You.
I know that Your Scriptures are faithful and true.
I ask You to accept me as a gift of Your grace,
And strengthen me, Lord, so I can run the good race.

I love You forever...

ADAM ZINSSER

Some people chase the silver and gold.
Others chase wisdom before they are old.
Mistakes will be made, yet roads will be laid.
Yet I chase the One that I'd never trade.

The One who chose to illustrate love.
When He came out of the water there was a beautiful dove
That descended from heaven to land upon Him.
He's the light of the world that will never go dim.

He's grace with a face, He's the true mercy seat.
He conquered death, never suffered defeat.
He's the Lamb who's a Lion, yet walked the earth as a Man.
When it came to my life, He's the one with the plan.

He is salvation, but He is also my King.
See, I wear His crown of thorns as my ring.
He showed me new life, and then He taught me love.
I walk on this earth, yet I chase Him above.

Most say they know Him, but in truth they are lost.
One thing He taught me is that we must count the cost.
The cost is a life of dying to self.
To give one's self away and stack up spiritual wealth.

To know Him is to show Him that you heard His call.
Let Him shine through your weakness whenever you fall.
I speak of the name above all other names.
The mighty name of Jesus, for there's no time for games.

Do you really know Him?

The Lord is my refuge, for He conquered death.
He got me off the needle that was pumping in meth.
He made me lie down in grass that was green.
He made me a miracle, something I had never seen.

He showed me love when life broke me down.
He found me homeless, and He gave me a crown.
From a dope fiend and a crook to a cross-bearing man.
No longer a child but part of His plan.

He did me like Lazarus and called me out of the tomb.
Yet He'd always been protecting me from way back in the
womb.
I just never saw it, for my eyes were shut tight.
I never liked living wrong, but I could never do right.

But He saved me, and He washed me of all I had done.
He said, "I've loved you forever, so I made you my son."
He comforts me and He shows me the things I should say.
One thing I know is that there's no other way.

Jesus is the way, but He is also salvation.
He's the only thing I talk about in any conversation.
He's all you'll ever need, and He'll set your soul on fire.
To me, He's just perfection. He's all that I desire.

He's my everything . . .

ADAM ZINSSER   83

Search my heart, Lord, and remove what is broken.
Teach me to live by the words You have spoken.
Open my eyes to what You want me to see.
Make my life more about You and less about me.

My only desire is to glorify You.
Help me forget all the wrong things I knew.
Blow on my spirit and just hold my hands.
Teach me to obey all Your commands.

You are the reason that I stand here today.
My heart only dances to the words that You say.
I carry this cross, and I lift up Your name
Because Your love has cleansed me of guilt and shame.

I offer my life here on this altar.
I depend on Your strength when I'm weak or I falter.
I come to You broken like an old shattered vase.
Just begging You, Jesus, please show me Your face.

You're my hero, my Savior, but You're also my friend.
I stand on Your promise of a glorious end.
I need You in ways that I can't even tell.
And I just wanna thank You for saving me from hell.

I worship You, Selah...

I want you to know that you're gonna fall.
But I promise I hear you whenever you call.
I'll pick you up, and I'll get you right.
See, I am your strength to keep fighting this fight.

I'll never leave you, and I'll never quit.
My love is eternal, so the pieces will fit.
I'll show you the way and bring you that peace.
I'll keep you pure and make the blessings increase.

I'll ease your pain from all of life's sorrows.
I'll teach you to smile, bring better tomorrows.
I'll give you hope where you never had any.
My thoughts about you are great and so many.

Just feel all my love and know that it's true.

What I did on that Cross, I did it for you.
I know that you're lost and hurting so much.
I just want to bless you with my gentle touch.

You are the reason I came up from the grave.

I don't want to hurt you; I just want to save
You from the heartache I know that you feel.
I'm asking you to believe that I'm truly real.

And that I love you...

Love always,

Jesus

I shall wait on the Lord, for He is my rock.
It's only His words of which I shall talk.
My life is a sacrifice that is holy and living.
My goal is to worship, to love, and to be giving.

I give myself away to the One who is true.
I am worshiping His name, and I'm right in front of you.
I'm telling you He's holy, He's the only One I need.
He is my everything, and for Him my heart bleeds.

Trials and tribulations are all in front of me.
But still I worship Jesus here on bended knee.
For nothing else compares to walking at His side.
He's the only One who heard me each time that I cried.

Worthy is the Lamb who for us has been slain.
Yet when He was resurrected, it became our gain.
So I will scream up to the heavens amongst women and men
That my life has been surrendered to the only true Amen!

For He is holy...

Thank You, Jesus...

I will worship You forever.

My God Is an Awesome God!

Most people don't know what it's like to just be dying.
They'll tell you that they do, but I promise that they're lying.
You wake up every day just stuck inside a cage.
You're drowning in depression, yet boiling with rage.

The years just pass you by, then it's decades that have passed.
The glimmer of hope,; well, it came and then it passed.
Violence is the norm, the hate is in the air.
Mail keeps on coming, but there's no one who really cares.

You're forgotten by the world as you stare out at the rain.
The only thing you know is that inside there's such pain.
Nowhere to look forward, the darkness haunts your soul.
Inside you are broken and needing to be whole.

This is where He found me, it's of Jesus that I speak.
He came to truly heal me, and He taught me how to seek.
He took away my sorrow and took away my strife.
The food that He would bring me He called the bread of life.

He took my heart of stone out and gave me one of gold.
He brought me out of prison and brought me to His fold.
So now I walk with Jesus, forever in His grace.
And before you bring my past up, just know He took my case.

He died for me and they

Dropped the charges . . .

It's called Deliverance!

Adam Zinsser

So where do I start when writing to You,
The most beautiful person that I ever knew?
Your love is so tender, Your strength is so great.
And You always show up, You're just never late.

You make beauty from ashes, You mend what is broken.
Everything came into existence by the words You have spoken.
You care for the ones that the world throws away.
And You always listen each time that I pray.

There is just no end to your grace and compassion.
You conquered sin in such a magnificent fashion.
You mock the wise with the foolish, the strong with the weak.
You promised to be found when I truly seek.

So I ran through the hills, and I fell on my face.
I begged for forgiveness, and You gave me grace.
You took me and washed me of all of my sin.
And You took all the pain from the places I've been.

I desire no one and nothing in this world more than You.
How wonderful Your love is; I had not a clue.
But You promised to be found when I seek with my heart.
Yet I never really realized I would get a fresh start.

New life, new spirit, new chance to help others.
I even got a new family that's my sisters and brothers.
But the greatest thing I got was a chance to be forgiven.
So to me, life minus You is not even worth living.

You saved me, and I worship You!

I come in the name of Jesus praying peace upon your day.
I plead the blood of Jesus over every word I say.
I bow my head to Jesus, for He alone is Lord.
I'm a soldier in His army, and the Bible is my sword.

I want you to know Jesus and love Him like I do.
I want you to surrender, for His love will make you new.
I want you to come boldly to His throne of grace.
I want to watch Him hold you, wiping tears from your face.

I want you to just seek Him and see His love is true.
At the Cross the world was called, yet the chosen are only few.
I want you to be humbled by a love that never quits.
So come and take this crown, for I promise that it fits.

Jesus is the answer to every problem that you had.
Jesus is true joy when your whole life you've been sad.
Jesus is your dreams all becoming oh so real.
I'm just in love with Jesus, so I'm telling you how I feel.

Jesus is the answer...

Sometimes I wonder what people see,
They hear me speak Jesus, but I know they judge me.
They look at my tats, they stare in my face.
They're quick to condemn, but where is God's grace?

I thought love was patient, that love was so kind.
Yet why amongst the body is it so hard to find?
I hear all the legalism and those chasing the law.
It tears at my heart, it leaves it so raw.

Faith without works is faith that is dead.
But did you hear the most important thing Jesus said?
He said love one another as I have loved you.
And in this you'll show the world that your love is true.

Jesus didn't condemn. No, he came to save.

But so many Christians put believers in the grave.
The hate, the judgment, the condemning of others.
They're just breaking down their sisters and brothers.

Jesus healed lepers, the blind, and the deaf.

He came to bring life, not judgment and death.
Yet people still persecute, thinking they do it for God.
That's not Christianity, that's a plague and a fraud.

Listen to His words and then pray up above.

Stop looking at the flesh, and magnify His love.
We're killing one another, not walking in the spirit.
A message from Jesus, and I hope that you hear it.

"If you do not know love, then you do not know God, for God is love" (1 John 4:8).

"For God did not send His Son into the world to condemn the world! But rather so that through Him the world might be saved" (John 3:17).

Legalism and Judgment is of Satan!

Relationships with Christ and Love for One Another is of God!

I'm Truly Grateful...

Today I'm just grateful for all that You've done.
Today I'm just grateful to be called Your son.
I'm grateful for how You changed all my ways.
The way You showed me that sin never pays.

From darkness to light, from blindness to sight.
Not by Your strength, Your power, but might.
I'm so far from perfect, but I'm so much better.
Lady Wisdom stayed calling but You let me get her.

You showed me things that I never knew;
That I could do anything. You made sure I grew.
Miracles on miracles is what I have seen.
To a true man of God from a broken, desperate fiend.

I once heard of You, but now I know who You are.
I know that You're with me, whether near or far.
I'm grateful for the way that you taught me true love.
Most of all, I'm just grateful that I'll see You above.

Yes, I'm grateful...

You are the Shepherd that died for Your sheep.
You rule my dreams when I go to sleep.
Your voice calms my spirit whenever I'm stressed.
Each day that begins I realize I'm blessed.

For You knew I was broken, but You gave me Your life.
You knew I had battled depression and strife.
You knew I had nightmares and so many fears.
You knew I'd been shattered for so many years.

You knew I was filthy, just drowning in sin.
You knew all the places in which I had been.
Still You had chosen to sanctify me.
Where I was blind for so long, You allowed me to see.

So where do I start when giving You praise?
How hard I do chase You and all Your ways.
You are Yahweh, yet You are the Son.
When I hear Your voice, it's to You that I run.

I bury Your laws deep down in my soul.
I give You my praise for Your love made me whole.
For God so loved the world that You died for me.
So I just want to thank You for setting me free.

I worship You . . .

ADAM ZINSSER

I'm proud to be cleansed by the precious love of Jesus.
I'm grateful for a God that protects us and always sees us.
You see, in all of my weaknesses, He becomes strong.
And He healed me inside when I had been hurting so long.

My God is my shelter, my fortress, my rock.
You'll only hear the name of Jesus when I talk.
I lift up His name, and I bask in His grace.
As far as the hatred, well, there is not a trace.

For He has shown me great things that I never knew.
He taught me to love myself, but to also love you.
He said, "There's no greater love than to lay your life down for a friend."
He said the plans that He has is to bring a glorious end.

From the heavens to the earth, I shall scream out His name.
Yeshua, I love you! I'm burning like a flame.
Your love is my love, and You are the king of all kings.
I chase You like David because for You my heart sings.

I shall write You these poems which are tokens of my love.
But one day I'll recite them in the heavens up above.
For You are my Master, and it's You that made me whole.
You are my prince of peace, the true lover of my soul.

Yes, I worship You and I shall chase You forever...in love.

Selah Master . . . I love You!

Greatness is defined by the One who is life.
The One who gives us peace and not so much strife.
He brings us comfort in times where it's such utter sorrow.
He is the Author of your greatest tomorrow.

Greatness is defined by the Lamb who's a Lion.
Anyone else is a fraud, and they're lying.
It's the One who gave it all for the world with their hate.
He died for His enemies, but that made him great.

Greatness is the One who chose to carry that Cross.
The One who gave us His blessing by taking that loss.
The One who turned water into sweet, tasty wine.
Greatness is Messiah, and I tell you, He's mine.

Greatness is the One who wore a crown of thorns.
The very One who named us before we were born.
See, He is the stairway that will take us all to heaven.
The One who rested in the tomb to hallow out day seven.

Greatness is the One who loves us oh so much.
The very One who craves to let you feel His touch.
Greatness is the One who died so we could win.
He was rose up from the dead to wash us of our sin.

That is greatness...

That's Jesus Christ of Nazareth!

Many people I know had never seen me smile.
For the select few that have known, it's sure been a while.
They're used to seeing me strung out on those streets
Or lost in the prisons, one of my many defeats.

They're used to the anger that had ruled from within.
They're used to seeing me blaspheme God with my sin.
They remember all the violence or never really knowing
If I'd make it to see forty, yet never see me growing.

But my God is a way maker when there simply is no way.
He defeats all the odds or what the world will say.
He takes all the ashes that have blown amongst the ground.
He brings them all to life and blesses those around.

I'm a product of His love and his never-ending grace.
I was chosen for His kingdom regardless of my face.
An example of His power turning darkness into light
I spent my life a blind man, yet look, He gave me sight.

I was chief of all the sinners, now I'm living for His glory.
I'm the hidden chapter He had hidden in His story.
I'm the one you were afraid of, now I magnify His love.
I was trapped inside of hell, now I'm headed up above.

So the smile that you see is all because of Him.
My face reflects His light, where my whole life it was dim.
It's not about religion or worshipping the law.
Cause what you see is Jesus, the greatest I ever saw.

I am a child of God . . .

I know that Your ways are different than mine.
Yet it's Your love for me that just makes me shine.
I struggle through life and wait on better days.
Yet so many times I feel I'm stuck in a maze.

I fall, and I fall, and I fall once again.
Yet I still worship You with this paper and pen.
From the dark, dark valleys and the shadows of death.
From gang life and violence, the needle and the meth.

You've taken me from places that were haunted with hate.
Yet you raised me up, and You're making me great.
No anger is left. Where it used to be crazy,
I'm up every day where I used to be lazy.

It's Your spirit that's in me, and it's got me on fire.
I'm just like an eagle soaring higher and higher.
I'm chasing You Lord with all that I am.
I'm screaming to the world that worthy is the Lamb.

I bow to You in reverence, and I give You my all.
See, with Your spirit in me, in the end I won't fall.
Not by Your might, Your strength, but Your spirit.
So my heart's crying out, and I pray that You'll hear it.

I worship You forever!

ADAM ZINSSER

He said, "I am the branch and you are the vine."
He said, "Give me your problems for the burden is mine."
He said, "I'm the Shepherd and you are my sheep.
For I catch every tear whenever you weep."

He said, "I am the door if you want to see heaven.
I am the one that hallowed out day seven.
It was me that knew you when you were still in the womb.
I hung on that Cross and walked out of the tomb.

"It was me in the garden in the very beginning.
I created the world, I got the world spinning.
I'm the Author of your heart no matter what you thought.
I was there for every battle that you've ever fought.

"I am the lover of your soul and I love you so much.
My only desire is that you feel my touch.
Not a moment goes by that I'm not thinking of you.
You see, I'm the good Shepherd that makes all things new.

"So pick up your cross and come follow Me.
I'll open the eyes of your heart so you'll see.
That you are so worthy, and that's why I died.
That I want you with me and that's why I cried."

I love you . . .

Love, Jesus Christ

My cross I will carry, Your love I will share.
My spirit is pure with me, there's no fear.
For You are beside me in all of my troubles.
Your strength that is in me helps me conquer struggles.

Your laws are a lamp that light up my path.
Your blood is my shield from sin and its wrath.
So I get up each day and pick up my shield.
My sword's in my hand, and I head to the field.

I give You my all and walk in Your light.
The world will condemn me, but I know that I'm right.
I walk through the valleys. I preach in the ghettos.
I rest in Your glory and run in Your meadows.

I sing Your praises and lift up Your name.
I'm telling the world that sin is no game.
I just want to thank You for all that You are
As I carry this cross from near and afar.

I worship You...

I know that I need You in all that I do.
I know You were with me in all I went through.
I know You gave me strength when I could not go on.
I just could not see the plan You had drawn.

One thing I've learned is Your love's never ending.
Blessings are something that You never stop sending.
You make a way when it seems I am lost.
I kept on sinning, yet You paid the cost.

So all I can do is get down on my knees,
Look up to the heavens so You'll hear my pleas.
Give You my worship, that's all of my praise.
And try to walk worthy of all Your ways.

I'll scream from the mountains that You are my Lord.
I'll march into battle full-fledged with my sword.
I'll preach from the gospel that speaks of Your peace.
I'll plant and water, You'll get the increase.

You are the Author of my faith and my love.
You are the One who sent me the dove.
Your spirit is in me, and the battle's been won.
For I am Your servant, Your friend, and Your son.

And I worship You forever.

To My Alpha and Omega...

To my Alpha and Omega, my beginning, and my end
Who chose me from the start as the one You will send.
To teach the world Your ways and all that You have spoken.
To come to heal the sick, the lost, and the broken.

You buried all Your laws deep down in my heart.
You found me in the darkness but gave me a new start.
You showed me that Your grace is always what I need.
You brought me to the Cross and showed me how You'd bleed.

You told me that I'm worthy of everything You did.
That I am Your creation, and I'm Your favorite kid.
The struggles that I've been through were for a certain reason.
The pain that I endured was only for a season.

You showed me that Your ways were higher that I see.
I thought that I was lost, but You had hold of me.
I thank You for Your love, compassion, and Your trust.
For me to follow You is simply just a must.

My words are simply worship that only You deserve.
My faith I have in You, there's simply no reserve.
Because living for me is just simply chasing You.
I worship You Christ Jesus, because only You are true.

I love You, Messiah...

The thing about Jesus is He's really that great.
He's always on time even if He's late.
He takes all our messes, working them all for the good.
Just look at the Cross, only two pieces of wood.

He's there for your darkest and hardest of times.
He takes all my words, and He creates rhymes.
But with a message that promises to sink to your soul,
The love that He gives us, it makes us feel whole.

He's the Alpha and Omega of things you see.
Through Him we can conquer all things and be free.
He shows you this peace that just blows your mind.
He says the one who truly seeks Me is the one that shall find.

He takes the world's trash, and He turns it to treasure.
He blesses our lives, and I mean beyond measure.
He forgives all our sins, and He washes us clean.
Then He lies down with us in grass that's so green.

I can never say enough about the things that He's done.
I could never outrun Him no matter how hard I run.
His goodness is forever, and His love is so pure.
See, I was dying with a sickness, but He was the cure.

The sickness was the sin that was all inside of me.
I saw Him in the garden, but I picked the wrong tree.
Yet He took me in His arms, and He showed me He's the way.
I'm just in love with Jesus, and that's all I've got to say.

I'm a proud follower of

Jesus Christ of Nazareth . . .

You taught me in Scripture to seek and I'll find.
You performed miracles, giving sight to the blind.
You turned sinners to saints and all with one touch.
You died on that Cross because You loved me so much.

It seems I couldn't see You till I thought I was dying.
I let the world fool me even though they were lying.
I bought the fool's gold, but it never looked good.
I knew You could save me, but I never thought You would

I thought I was trash that no one desired.
I was broken inside, and I knew I was tired.
I never felt loved or like I even belonged.
From my very first day, I felt I'd been wronged.

I mean, who takes a child and just throws him away?

Why would they leave you when you ask them to stay?
I never had a family or a place to call home.
I was just a statistic that no one had known.

But the day I met you, it's like I knew who You were.
My whole life I was broken, yet You were the cure.
You showed me a love that just wouldn't quit.
I had always been shattered, but You made the pieces fit.

So my love for You is a love that keeps growing.
The wisdom that You gave me is definitely worth knowing.
My loyalty to You is simply unreal.
I only wanna worship You as I get down and kneel.

Because I love You, Jesus.

ADAM ZINSSER   103

Enjoying the very blessings that Christ has bestowed upon me. This is my bike that I named King Jesus!

When I'm out there on the road, the wind blowing on my face,
I'm looking all around me, just reminded of God's grace.
The beauty of the skies and the trees that are all around
It's a picture that He's painted that I had come and found.

When I'm rolling down the highway, my heart just simply sings.
It's like Jesus came and touched me and gave me eagles' wings.
Not too many people could relate to how I feel.
It's like Jesus made my Harley so I'd know His love is real.

He speaks to my spirit when I'm on that open road.
They ask me why I love Him, well, it's just the love He showed.
For love is not a word, but really, it's an action.
It's making sure that person is feeling satisfaction.

Jesus knew my passion was riding on them bikes.
He knows the things I don't want, but He also knows my likes.
So this is how He blessed me, He put me on a glide.
He gave me this sweet Harley, and for me He had died.

Yeah, He really loves me.

Just riding with Jesus.

ADAM ZINSSER

I've seen so much hate, anger, and hurt.
Almost everyone I was in the gang with is asleep in the dirt.
I grew up in the prisons where I was trapped in that hell.
The blood would be everywhere, but there's no one to tell.

They say this world is crazy, but it's really not so bad.
It does get depressing, and at times it leaves you sad.
But I came up in the jungles where dreams you just can't sell.
You look inside that prison cell, it's another life that fell.

I've seen wars and so much violence, it broke me down inside.
The man whose blood you see, well, I promise that he died.
He'd never get to make it out to see the light of day.
They're murdered in these prisons, but that's the price they pay.

Those are things you see each day that you are trapped.
Minds are always breaking and necks are getting snapped.
The stabbings are aplenty, life just holds no weight.
But if they don't know Christ Jesus, they'll never see the gate.

Jesus chose to save me. He sets the captives free.
That's why I choose to worship and pray down on my knee.
Cause that blood that's in that cell, thank God it wasn't mine.
See, I gave my life to Christ, and for Him I shall shine.

The things that I went through.

You came and found me in the darkest of places.
I was stuck and surrounded by the darkest of faces.
The blood, the sin, the hatred, and death.
I had a needle in my arm as I pushed in the meth.

The pain was unbearable with the guilt and the shame.
When I first started using, they said it's "the game."
But the game had gotten old, and it was for keeps.
See, whatever one sows is just what he reaps.

I saw many die, and I touched broken souls.
I used dirty needles and smoked dirty bowls.
I robbed many people with greed and a gun.
Every time I got high, I would take off and run.

The demons were all there, just following me around.
Everyone was screaming, but I couldn't hear a sound.
My body was in ruins, and my mind was simply shattered.
I lost everyone that loved me or anything that mattered.

This is where You found me, completely void of hope.
Sitting in the county detoxing of the dope.
You wrapped Your arms around me and lifted me above.
You showed me who You are, and that is simply love.

So now it's four years later, and I'm completely new.
I'm sober and I'm healthy, and I'm only preaching You.
I'm humbled and I'm grateful for everything You've done.
Now I am Your servant, but most importantly, Your son.

You left the ninety-nine for me ... thank You, Jesus, for saving me.

ADAM ZINSSER

I'm Reaching for a Miracle...

I'm reaching for a miracle. I'm praying for Your touch.
I'm praying that I'll reach You. I'm needing You so much.
I need to feel Your spirit. I'm needing to just heal.
So I'm bowing in Your presence. For You, I'll gladly kneel.

I'm begging for forgiveness for all the things I've done.
I'm coming in surrender, no longer will I run.
I'm asking You to show me all that I need to know.
To guide me in the spirit, so that in You I will grow.

I know Your love is true, that it will set me free.
I know that when You died, You did it all for me.
I just wanna know Your power, Your power of Resurrection.
I wanna know You better, Your love and Your affection.

Just blow up on my spirit and speak Your truth to me.
Break the chains upon me and set my spirit free.
Give me that new heart that makes me follow You.
And I will always worship the only One that's true.

I will worship You 4-ever...

I just want You to know that You own my heart.
I pray that our spirits will not drift apart.
Because I need You to guide me through all my days.
I need You to know that You leave me amazed.

The things that You do just leave my mind blown.
Since I have met You, I really have grown.
My heart's become pure, and my spirit is true.
When it comes to my life, well, it's all about You.

I chase You in the spirit, and I'm with You in my dreams.
It keeps on getting better, at least that's how it seems.
I rest on Your chest, where our hearts beat as one.
I stand upon Your promise that Calvary is done.

It's deeper than Your laws or the words I read each day
When I open Your Word or I hit my knees to pray.
This is all a romance, it's the best I ever knew.
I'm giving You my all in everything I do.

You are my beginning, You showed me what I need.
You showed me what true love is when You chose to bleed.
And this is what I've realized, that You are simply grace.
As I lay down in my bed, and I dreamed I kissed Your face.

I love You, Messiah...

Just thankful for Your love.

I decided to wake up and just write you all a letter,
to the ones who are lost and think things can't get better.
I want you to know that there's always hope.
There's life past the anger, the sadness, and dope.

I want you to realize that it's a choice that you make,
when you get to the point where you just want to break.
See, the ways of this world will only leave you hurt;
I have so many friends who now sleep in the dirt.

The drugs and the booze, the heartaches and pain;
I remember being homeless and sleeping in the rain.
The depression was suffocating, the anxiety was hell.
Yet, to be quite honest, there was no one to tell.

I was breaking and breaking more every day.
I had no relationship with Christ, so I just didn't pray.
Penitentiary, then detox, psyche meds, then meth.
Everywhere I was looking, I saw heartbreak and death.

I gave up my years to this madness right here.
I could never feel a victory cause I was stuck in the fear.
Finally, one day I just knew it had to end.
I knew that I was broken, and I just wanted to mend.

So I gave my life to Jesus and asked about His way.
I asked Him to stay in my heart, and He promised He'd stay.
First, He changed my mind and the things that I would do.
Then He healed me of the pain of the things I'd been through.

He taught me how to love and to do the things that are right.
He opened up my eyes and truly gave me sight.

So my letter is to the ones who are out there that are shattered,
My message is from Jesus. He said you've always mattered.
He wants you to come and lay your burdens at His feet.
He's the only answer to fight off that defeat.
I'm only an example of the richness of His grace.
I promise that He'll fix you, put a smile on your face.

I live in this world, but it's not where I'm from.
I won't ever march to the beat of its drum
For I'm from the heavens, and I'm just passing through.
I'm a son of Messiah, I thought that you knew.

I'm here to speak life and to heal all the broken.
I'm here to repeat all that Jesus has spoken.
I'm here to shine light into a world that is lost.
To bring forth redemption because He paid the cost.

I'm just a voice in the wilderness that's calling.
I'm trying to catch the ones that are falling.
I'm bringing God's grace in the name of Messiah.
And for those who are seeking, I'm taking you higher.

The blessings I speak of, they won't ever stop.
We pick up our cross, and we don't let it drop.
The love that I offer will heal those who are shattered.
The name that I speak of is the one that mattered.

I know where I came from but also where I'm going.
The hardest part about this is really just the knowing.
But the faith that I have is not ever to be shaken.
I'm headed to heaven, this is the journey I'm making.

I'm just passing through.

To My Love, El Shaddai...

I'm writing this letter because You make me better.
If I had Your address, well, I'd send You a letter.
Each and every day, I'd send You my love.
For now, I write a poem and I whisper it above.

For the way that You changed me, I can never explain.
The way that You freed me from so much of the pain.
The depression that plagued me is all simply gone.
But this was the plan in which You had drawn.

You took a wretched sinner, and You raised him for Your glory.
You took a dying leper and made him part of Your story.
You took me from addiction, and You blessed me with peace.
You held me oh so close and made my heartbeat increase.

Like David, I will chase You until my last breath.
Like Paul, I will promote You, then I will conquer death.
Like Abraham, I will follow You across the whole earth.
Like the angels, I will worship You for Your miracle birth.

I know what You did that day inside of me.
You took a dying blind man, and You allowed me to see.
You took a heart of stone and replaced it with flesh.
You made a masterpiece where there had been a mess.

So what can I do but preach from Your Word?
I have to keep repeating the beautiful things my heart heard.
Because in You is life, and that life is worth living.
It is the guilt of salvation and the art of forgiving.

I worship You forever, Selah...
Your faithful servant forever.

ADAM ZINSSER

Simply Grateful...

Today I want You to know how grateful I am.
I want to tell the world that worthy is the Lamb.
I want them to know how magnificent You are.
That You know the name of each and every star.

I want to say thank You for everything You do.
For all of the nightmares that You got me through.
For protecting me through the years that I blasphemed Your name.
For washing me clean of my sins and my shame.

I doubted Your glory, and I mocked You for fun.
I hated Your creations, and I thought I was done.
But You opened my eyes, and You softened my heart.
You chose to resurrect me instead of tearing me apart.

You were patient and kind, and You never stopped believing.
You whispered in my spirit that You were never leaving.
You held me in Your arms, and You wiped all my tears.
It was You who protected me through all my prison years.

So I'm simply grateful for everything that You did.
In all my darkest years when I ran and hid.
Now I am surrendered to Your love and Your compassion.
This heart of mine's on fire, and it's filled with such passion.

I will serve You and praise You for the rest of my days.
I'm promoting Your kingdom with Your heavenly ways.
Because I never deserved this love that You gave me
Or the fact that You found me, and You chose to save me.

I'm simply grateful...

I love You, and I worship You forever and ever, Jesus!

Some people grow up in a beautiful home.
They live like kings or queens on their throne.
They're raised up with Jesus, and they live a great life.

Then there are others like me who are born into war.
Everywhere they knocked, people slammed the door.
Rejected and neglected, no trust or even love.
There was no one to count on when push came to shove.

You're raised up on the streets or many institutions.
You're hungry and you're broken, but there are no solutions.
Your world is always dark with no one there to tell.
People preach this heaven, but your whole life's been hell.

That's what I had been through. It was darkness for forty years.
I never saw the hope, just brokenness and tears.
Until one day He touched me, and then I saw His light.
I felt the hope within, and the world became so bright.

Ashes turned to beauty, and He showed me what it meant.
To finally have salvation. He said I was heaven sent.
The night became the day, and my battles were finally won.
It's crazy how it took the darkness to finally meet the Son.

But He saved me . . .

Thank you, Christ Jesus . . .

If I Ever...

Lord, if I ever seem ungrateful, just know that I'm not.
I know in my spirit that it is my heart You bought.
I know that You found me when I was just shattered,
When I had lost everything in my life that mattered.

I know that the drugs had clouded my brain.
I know I was going crazy from all the pain.
The life that I had known was hurt with many fears.
Yet I never even realized You had captured all my tears.

I hurt so many others because I was hurting inside.
The pain was just unbearable, but I couldn't seem to hide.
I didn't wanna be here, and I was hurting so much.
But then You changed it all with a simple little touch.

You showed me that You loved me like no one had before.
You whispered in my heart, and Your words said so much more.
You lifted up Your hand where they had driven the nail.
You told me You adore me and that Your love for me is real.

So if I seem ungrateful, I'm really just ashamed.
See, the love I have for You, it will always be untamed.
I am thankful for the blessings that You give me every day.
And I swear I'll always love You till I live my final day.

Yes, I'm truly grateful...

Simply grateful for His love.

I used to wonder if I would ever find love,
If someone would be there when push came to shove.
I wondered if I'd feel that compassionate touch,
Or even hear that person say they love me so much.

Broken heart and shattered dreams were all I ever knew.
The things that I would dream of, I'd never get to do.
The trauma that I went through was more than I could bear.
But it doesn't ever help to claim that life isn't fair.

So I gave up on the notion of simply being desired.
Every job I ever got, well, I'd always end up fired.
It's hard to live this life alone and just so broken.
It's like begging for a breath, but instead you're just stuck choking.

But then I met my Jesus, and He changed the way I felt.
No longer did it matter the hand that I was dealt.
His love had simply changed me, so beautiful and pure.
See, I spent my whole life dying, but His love had proved the cure.

So now I'm repping Jesus no matter where I go.
His love is what I preach, cause I want the world to know
That what He did inside me, He will do it all for you.
He's simply just amazing, and I know he loves you too.

I'm just in love with Jesus!

A child that Jesus loves.

I am the one that You found in the grave.
I am that sinner that You chose to save.
I am the one that You carried that Cross for.
I am the one that You showed the door.

I was lost in my transgressions, drowning in sin.
I was fighting for my life, but I just couldn't win.
I was drowning in the water, and You took me by the hand.
You told me that You loved me, but I didn't understand.

See, I couldn't understand why You wanted me.
When You looked into my heart, what exactly did You see?
When You looked into my future, did it look just like my past?
And if You chose to save me, would the blessing really last?

Yet You had known the questions that were weighing down my mind.
You were full of pure compassion, patient and so kind.
You told me that You had me, and You would make me new.
You showed me that Your love was genuine and true.

So my journey had begun, that day I fell in love.
There was no more looking down, for my future was above.
Now I am walking with You, a soldier for Your nation.
I am blessing all the world with the secret of salvation.

I'm not drowning anymore. See, I'm walking on that water.
I'm living for Your kingdom, and I'm building for my daughter.
So these are the words of worship for the greatest to ever live
To tell You that I love You, and my life is what I give.

You are my everything!

As long as I'm breathing, I'll walk with You.
I hold on to Your promise to make all things new.
You breathed on my spirit and You proved who You are.
You took me from darkness. Now I shine like a star.

When I'm weak, You are strong, and You gift me with vision.
You showed me Your true church has no division.
You showed me the secret of peace in my mind.
You said if I'm seeking, I'm promised to find.

So here I am, humbled and broken to pieces.
I'm asking for Your love so that my faith increases.
I'm asking You to touch me with the tip of Your finger
So I can dance with Your spirit, and I pray it will linger.

Your ways are too great, and Your love is too sweet.
I wanna sit in Your presence and bask at Your feet.
The Cross that You carried held all of my sin.
You even protected me in the hell where I had been.

So this life that I live is a life that You gave.
You're the reason I'm breathing and not dead in the grave.
For that, I will lift Your name up so high.
I can't deny You because I can't live a lie.

I worship You, Yeshua . . .

Many people ask me who He is to me.
They ask when I pray, just what do I see?
They ask if He's real, and does He know who they are,
And if He lives in heaven, why is He off so far?

They ask why there's sin and so many dying,
Or why do these preachers spend Sundays just lying?
They ask why the rules are so hard to follow
And tell me God's story is just too hard to swallow.

My response to these statements goes something like this:
They are simple but true, so you don't wanna miss.
I tell them that Jesus is certainly real,
That salvation's a reality, not something they feel.

I say He's in heaven, but He's also right here.
I say His laws are life, and they're nothing to fear.
I tell them that pastors are not all that bad,
That there are false prophets and that much is sad.

I tell them that the spirit will never mislead.
He's holy and He's truth, that we must take heed.
I tell them that sin is killing off many,
But so are the ones that won't spare a penny.

I tell them that Jesus is life, and He's love,
That He created everything down here and above.
I tell them that Christ will return here one day
That He hears their cries whenever they pray.

I tell them that to me, He's the best that existed,
That I hope I answered all the questions they listed.
That's all that He asks is we trust and believe
And to know that the enemy will always deceive.

I know what you think when you look at me.
You think to yourself there is no way this can be.
You remember the days I was so full of hate,
When I walked around thinking I was so great.

You remember the anger and aggression I had.
The way I hurt those around me, leaving them sad.
The way that I stole, deceived, and I lied.
When I left being around you, you wished I had died.

You remember the violence, the hurt, and the tears.
You remember the way I fed off your fears.
I never would smile or say anything nice.
I had a gun and a needle. I was shooting up ice.

Well, I just wanna tell you, that's not me anymore.
I had an encounter with Christ, and He showed me much more.
He took out the heart that was made of pure stone,
And He told me that I was never alone.

His love has transformed me like you wouldn't believe.
He taught me integrity and to never deceive.
He taught me to smile, and He taught me true love.
The best thing about it is, I'm headed above.

He made me completely new.

A new creation . . .

ADAM ZINSSER

My message to you is simply to try it.
If you think that He's fake, well, you don't have to buy it.
But give it a try and see that He's good,
My only advice is that you really should.

Why live blind when you could have sight?
Why keep on losing when it's not your fight?
You're losing so much and running out of time.
Without Christ in your life, you'll just never climb.

With Christ, you will soar through the sky with no fear.
He will never leave you. He will always be here.
He'll take all your heartbreaks and turn them to laughter.
He not only gives life but a great hereafter.

He teaches you things that you just never knew.
He's asking for a relationship, but it's all up to you.
You can stay in the darkness and drown in your pain.
Or you can trust in the rainbow that follows the rain.

He loves you so much, if you would only believe.
So come to the Cross and you'll feel relieved.
His love is forever, and His grace is for all.
I just want to invite you to answer His call.

Trust and see that He's good.

I just want to thank You for waking me up today.
I'm not sure what to do but I know I wanna pray.
I want to let You know that You are everything to me.
I also want to ask You to show me how to see.

What I mean is to see the things that You want me to know.
Breathe upon my spirit, so I'll continue to grow.
I want to heal the broken and show them what You are.
I want to feed the hungry, whether near me or afar.

I wanna show them Jesus like they've never seen before.
I want to feed their spirits, where they'll chase You for
some more.
I'll show them why David loved You so much.
Like the woman who was bleeding, I need to feel Your
touch.

I want to walk beside You and look to see Your smile.
I want to show the world that Jesus is my style.
You took me from the darkness, then changed me to a light.
I want the world to feel You as You hold them all so tight.

This is just a prayer to tell You what I feel
To tell You that I'll worship You, and I'm not ashamed to
kneel.
To tell You, You are holy and the greatest to ever live.
To repent of all my sins and just ask You to forgive.

AMEN . . . I love You, Messiah.

This is me strung out on meth in the death grips of Satan.

To me, it all starts and finishes with one name...
Jesus Christ!

**I find my only true rest in the Lord.
He is my Shelter and my Rock.**

At some point in time you just have to hit your knees and surrender. You have to ask the Lord to help you undo this mess. This was that point for me.

This is a 9 year old me. Very damaged
but not yet tainted by the enemy.

**This is my big brother and mentor, David Rose.
He has been such a blessing to my life.**

The only thing I can tell you is that Christ is so worthy of our worship. He will forever be worthy.

**Christ is simply my Everything.
There's no other way to put it!**

I got the privilege of going back to minister to
and encourage the men on the same prison unit
I served, 3 of my 24 plus years of prison time.

Most people will never truly understand how much Messiah means to me. But it'll never stop me from chasing Him like young David in the scriptures!

**Jesus Christ to me is my only Way,
only Truth, and my only Life!**

**Wearing His love, my cross, and a smile!
Thank you Jesus for making me a miracle!**

My joy is found simply in knowing thy King of all Kings.
And knowing that no one can pluck me out of His Hand.

Adam's life began long before he was actually born, when a young girl named Penny decided to experiment with drugs, and a kid named Mike took his first taste of alcohol. Penny became an addict, and Mike an alcoholic. They got together and produced three children; Adam was the youngest. Mike became a mean drunk who couldn't support his two children. He left Penny sometime around the birth of Adam, and when the cost of providing for her three children and supporting her addiction became too much, Penny left her children with a relative and went off to support her addiction. The biological relatives had young families of their own already and could not support three additional children. They made the difficult decision to turn the children over to social services. Being abandoned by the parents they loved was hard on all the children, but Adam was only nine months old. He suffered an emotional reaction so severe he had to be hospitalized.

The children were separated and placed in a series of foster homes that were not always well monitored. In one placement, the children reported that their baby brother (Adam) was being kept in a cage and fed dog food. This was verified, and the children were moved. They eventually were placed in the very small home of a devout Christian who had five biological children and had adopted two girls with Down syndrome. Adam and his siblings made ten children in that very small three-bedroom house. When the children were toddlers, it worked, but six years later the children were much bigger and the youngest of the biological boys who shared a room with Adam and his brother Mike were entering puberty and exploring their sexual orientations. It was not a healthy environment or situation.

During this period efforts were being made to reunite the children with their biological parents. Three times the children were told court dates had been set to give their parents the chance to get them back, and three times their parents failed to show up. Finally, when the children were six, eight, and ten they were released for adoption, but they were eight, ten, and twelve when they were placed with the people Adam considers his real family in Colorado. All three children flourished from the moment they set foot in their new home with us in what was supposed to be their forever family.

The elementary school they attended was right around the corner. It was on the President's list of 100 Best Elementary Schools in the country. Indian Ridge Elementary offered all kinds of extra-curricular activities, and Adam wanted to do everything. We limited him to three activities per quarter, and he excelled at everything. The school had a wonderful music program, and Adam chose to learn the French horn. Within months, he was playing with award-winning children's orchestras. The sound he could produce on the French horn was incredible.

We had a piano, and Adam taught himself to play by ear. The eight-year-old Adam, who was afraid to get into the baby pool with his soon-to-be father at his side, took a three-week swimming class, joined the community swim team, and was soon winning medals. While the children were in foster care, their scores on standardized tests had hovered between the tenth and twentieth percentiles. After one year in what was to be their forever family, their scores jumped to between the sixtieth and eightieth percentiles.

After more than a year of supervised placement, an adoption date for the three children was set, and the soon-to-be new family made arrangements to come to Colorado from St. Louis and Oklahoma to attend the ceremony and welcome the new grandchildren, nieces, nephews, and cousins to a large stable extended family. The children had remained in contact with both the biological family and the foster family in Massachusetts. All were happy for the children, but two days before the adoption was to take place, the agency in

Massachusetts demanded yet another home study. It was not possible to comply before the court date. The adoption was postponed indefinitely. The extended family had gathered, but the children, who had been rejected by biological parents and who could not become a part of their foster family, were not allowed to join the family who loved and wanted them.

After the adoption was blocked, Adam's sister decided she wanted to return to foster care in Massachusetts where she expected her biological mother would return for her. She went back, but she decided she was going to bring her brothers with her. The boys announced that they didn't care if Barbara wanted to go back; they liked it where they were and they wanted to stay. They were told by the agency in Massachusetts that wasn't an option; they were to be returned to Massachusetts foster care (where, in all probability, the window for adoption was closed). When school ended that year, Adam and Mike came home crying. Adam explained that all their friends were going home to their parents and families, but he and Mike didn't have a home or parents. What he didn't say, but probably realized, was that he and Mike could be separated.

Carl and I and the boys woke up every morning for at least seven months not knowing if the boys would be with us when the children would normally go to bed. It was the '80s. We had been moderately affluent; however, my husband was a research scientist who made his living through the seismic processing branch of the oil industry. When the oil industry collapsed, it circled the wagons in Houston. The stock market collapsed, and we lost $40,000 overnight. The seismic processing company my husband and two other men had started couldn't make payroll, so he separated himself from the company and began consulting and processing from our basement.

Although we had a four-bedroom house in a wonderful subdivision in Houston served by another good school district, we loved our children and had committed ourselves to providing them a forever family. The children's social workers in Colorado were familiar with the remarkable adjustment the children had made, and outside of us, they were the children's support system. We were afraid to move back to Texas before the adoption could be finalized. The stunt the agency in Massachusetts had pulled to preserve the revenue they were receiving from the state was devastating to the children, but the emotional stress Carl and I experienced was compounded by the financial stress of being trapped in a state where neither one of us could take advantage of our educations to earn a living. This arbitrary demand they had placed on us was made with no concern for the children. What we could once easily afford became extremely difficult to maintain.

Initially, when Carl began consulting, we had more than one hundred clients. Within a year, more than eighty clients had gone out of business. I was not certified to teach in Colorado. We literally were eking along on credit, but we hired a lawyer ($80,000 that we couldn't afford). I suspected the state agency in charge of child welfare had no clue what was going on and the horrendous anxiety they were using taxpayer money to inflict on helpless children, so I began a writing campaign to every conceivable person who might have the power to intervene on behalf of the children. I was just starting my letter to the governor (who happened to be running for president) when the news came that the children were cleared or we were cleared to finalize the adoption.

It was a date I have long since forgotten, but I will never forget the excitement in Adam's eyes when the limousine pulled into the driveway to take us to court. We hired a magician for an adoption party, which was attended by all the boys' friends and other supportive adults in their lives. A good time was had by all. Adam and his brother Michael officially became Zinssers, and Adam Robert opted to change his name legally to incorporate his father's middle name. From that day forward, he became Adam Clement Zinsser.

We were finally able to return to Texas where I could earn enough to support us, but it was not smooth sailing. It meant leaving a neighborhood where the children had many friends and teachers who knew and supported them. It meant leaving the church where they were known and supported. We left on Christmas Eve with two children, a dog, two cats, and two vehicles. Adam and I led in the car, while Carl and Mike followed in the van with the dog, two cats, and the junk we brought with us. We made it to my parents' house in Oklahoma on Christmas Day. Carl remained in Oklahoma, where we still had clients, and I took the children on to Houston so I could get them started in school by the beginning of the second semester. Both boys were in middle school in Texas.

When we reached our once beautiful home, the house was in shambles. The tenants had not watered the foundations regularly, if at all. The clay soil had constricted; the foundation had sunk and cracked. The house was uninhabitable. The doors, once opened, wouldn't close, let alone lock. I called Carl, and he got back as soon as he could, but that meant abandoning the possibility of future income. We were carrying about $70,000 in credit card debt and had no way of paying for the massive foundation work that had to be done before the house could be restored. I got the children into school. My parents borrowed on an insurance policy to cover the cost of the foundation repair (fifty-seven piers were needed to level the house), and once that was done Carl and I could set about repairing the rest of the damage ourselves.

As soon as Carl got back to Houston, I began substituting while he continued the research that would pull us out of debt seven years later. By March I had a permanent fulltime teaching position in one of the most dangerous middle schools in Houston, but we needed my salary and insurance benefits.

The children were adjusting to school. Summer was coming, and they hadn't made any real friends yet, so Carl and I decided to send both boys on different school-sponsored summer trips. Mike toured the East Coast on a trip that brought him close to his sister, and Adam toured Texas. It was a good way for the boys to meet friends and begin to learn in a healthy way that they didn't necessarily need us while understanding that they had a home and parents to come back to.

They were reaching the ages when I knew they would be exposed to drugs and peer pressure, so I began to warn them of choices they were going to face. Adam assured me that I didn't have to worry about him and his brother because they had seen what addiction had done to their parents, but what neither he nor I realized at that time was what their addiction had done and would do to them and every person whose lives they touched. Penny and Mike had passed on to their children a genetic predisposition to addiction. For Mike and Adam, the gateway drug was nicotine. It is not uncommon for teenagers to experiment with anything and everything their parents warn them against, and peer pressure is a powerful thing. Once they tried cigarettes, it was a simple step to marijuana. Both Mike and Adam were instantly addicted.

Adam on drugs is extremely dangerous. As a child he had become a master manipulator. As a teenage addict, he became a master instigator. He was strong, amoral, and reckless. By the age of fourteen, he was a serious addict. He had lost interest in his music and school. Lying and stealing became a way of life. From marijuana, Adam moved on to probably every other drug available. When he got into trouble at school, I moved him to the school where I taught, but he skipped classes there too and brought weed to school. Soon, he was totally out of control. He was expelled from the school where I taught.

Adam's behavior was both frightening and humiliating. I sought help from everyone and anyone who had seen a teenager on drugs. We sent the boys on an Outward-Bound program and a military school summer program. When Adam's behavior landed him in trouble with the law, I convinced the judge to put him in a rehab program. Nothing worked. He dropped out of high school after the tenth grade. We sought counseling for him, but were told that he could not be helped. My doctor began treating me for depression. I became the undisputed authority on what didn't work. In spite of my repeated failures, and the disturbing diagnosis from a highly regarded psychologist, I refused to give up until the third or fourth time Adam found himself in prison.

Adam writes prolifically about all the horrible things he did during that period of his life. I have done my best to repress those memories. I dwell only on the happy memories and the laughter we shared. Adam has a wonderful sense of humor and he is a really funny guy. I can attest to his confessions, but I find it difficult to accept any credit he gives me for helping him. Motherhood was not my forte, and nothing I did helped him deal with the scars of rejection, insecurity, abuse, and addiction.

Through all my failures, I learned two things I can share with other people who have come to know the despair that comes from watching a child or loved one suffer the pain of addiction. First, you can't help someone who won't help himself or herself. The second thing came from something Adam said to me recently when he was helping a friend get into a Christian sober living program. He pointed out that I had always been there every time he needed material things like clothes, food, and shelter, but none of those things had worked because I couldn't provide the support that comes from others who have experienced the trauma of addiction. He is only partially right, that support is incredibly important, but the real support that turned Adam's life around came from God.

I started by telling you that Adam's life began with the decisions and choices his biological parents made before he was born, which is true, but if you believe in God, you realize that He is with you at or before the moment of conception. Miracles abound all around us; some we take for granted, and others blow us away. Adam is a miracle I never expected; it blew me away. Thirty years of anger, hatred, and violence exacerbated by drug addiction have been melted away by God's love, mercy, and grace. Adam turned to the Bible when there was nowhere left to go, and he found Jesus. He sought to understand Jesus and all the people of the Old and New Testaments. He sought to connect their knowledge and experiences to the trials and tribulations he and many of us face in our everyday lives.

Adam is still Adam, and he faces new frustrations (as we all do) regularly. After venting, he turns to the Bible for guidance. Adam has a Scripture for everything, and he has a gift for showing us how the Scriptures can help twenty-first century Christians. I have known the story of the Prodigal Son since my childhood, but when I met the man my child has grown up to be, I felt and understood the joy of the father in that story. The only important thing the author would want you to know about his life is that the miracle God worked in his life, He can and will work in anyone's life who will let Him. Those who are broken can be healed as Adam has, and the joy of the father in the Prodigal Son can be felt when the prayers of those who have failed in their efforts to help those they love will know and understand the father of the prodigal son. I hope what Adam has learned and shares with you can help you find the peace and joy he and I have found through God's mercy and grace.

Judie Zinsser

Milton Keynes UK
Ingram Content Group UK Ltd.
UKHW050658261123
433299UK00004B/12